THE BOOK OF
HOME DESIGN

USING IKEA HOME FURNISHINGS

THE BOOK OF HOME DESIGN

USING IKEA HOME FURNISHINGS

ANOOP PARIKH

CONSULTANT EDITOR JOANNA COPESTICK

SPECIAL PHOTOGRAPHY TREVOR RICHARDS

HarperStyle
An Imprint of HarperCollins*Publishers*

THE BOOK OF HOME DESIGN.
Copyright © 1995 by Inter IKEA Systems B.V.
and Weidenfeld & Nicolson. All rights
reserved. Printed in Italy. No part of this book
may be used or reproduced in any manner
whatsoever without written permission except
in the case of brief quotations embodied in
critical articles and reviews. For information,
address HarperCollins Publishers, Inc.,
10 East 53rd Street, New York, NY 10022.

HarperCollins books may be purchased for
educational, business or sales promotional use.
For information, please write: Special Markets
Department, HarperCollins Publishers, Inc.,
10 East 53rd Street, New York, NY 10022.

FIRST EDITION
Library of Congress Cataloging-in-Publication
Data available upon request.

ISBN 0-06-273405-9

95 96 97 98 99 PTR 10 9 8 7 6 5 4 3 2 1

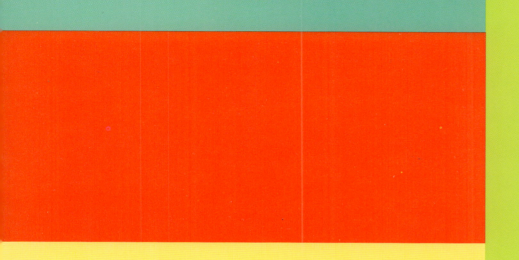

To Danny, for showing the way.

Editorial Direction JOANNA COPESTICK
Design and Art Direction MERYL LLOYD
Picture Editor NADINE BAZAR
Illustrator PAUL BRYANT
Typesetting IAN MUGGERIDGE

Special Photography TREVOR RICHARDS
Photographic Styling ANOOP PARIKH
Assisted by FIONA CRAIG-McFEELY

NOTE
Please note that not all the home furnishings
featured in this book are available from
IKEA. Those which are featured may not be
available from IKEA stores at all times.
For a list of countries in which you will find
IKEA, please refer to page 200.

CONTENTS

FOREWORD

The Book of Home Design sets out to prove, once and for all, that you can live stylishly and comfortably on a limited budget. Whether you are decorating your first home, adapting it to suit a growing family, or simply looking for fresh ideas, this book shows you how to analyze your needs and establish your priorities. It provides you with the information you need to create welcoming, attractive, practical and healthy spaces in every part of your home.

I am thrilled to have had IKEA's help in preparing this book. I have long admired their ability to bring simple, well-designed products within everyone's reach. IKEA is the only home furnishings store in the world which encourages people to create a look that is uniquely their own. The company looks forward continually, trying to anticipate our future needs and habits. But it never loses sight of the fact that its roots lie in the Swedish design tradition, which is synonymous with comfort, practicality, harmony and good value.

This book will, I hope, make it clear that there is no 'correct' way to decorate your home; instead, it aims to show you how to recognize, understand and choose from the many options available to you at each stage of the decorating process. The tone of the text is practical, but the pictures are amongst the most inspiring to be found anywhere. I hope it serves as a useful reminder that the central function of home design is not to impress one's friends and neighbours, but to create a better environment for yourself and your loved ones.

Anoop Parikh.

A Fresh Start

Moving into a new home is always exciting, but never more so than when you are doing it for the first time. It doesn't matter whether your first home is rented or bought, you know it is going to change your life; and you want the decor to reflect the fact that it is all yours, as fast as possible.

But where do you begin? When you are working to a limited budget, one of the easiest ways to start is to carry out a quick cover-up to create a plain or neutral backdrop in each room. In a living room, for example, you might decide to paint over the wallpaper and cover the inherited armchairs and sofa with white sheets so that your favourite possessions can grab all the attention.

The other option is to get used to the place first: to get under its skin before making any dramatic decisions. Allow yourself time to see if the shape of a room offers up clues as to how it should be designed. Either way, it is important to highlight a room's good points such as windows or an attractive fireplace, and make the best of bad points, rather than pretend they don't exist. Ugly features don't disappear; they need to be played down, or artfully disguised.

Once you are happy with the backdrop, it becomes easier to work out what your furnishing needs are. Every home needs certain basic items. These are: a decent bed; somewhere to sit – be it a couple of bean bags or a sofa; somewhere to hang and store your clothes; a suitable table and chair if you work at home, and shelves, cupboards or boxes for your remaining possessions.

You will inevitably have to find ways to give rather disparate groups of furniture a more harmonious feel. Giving them a theme, perhaps by painting them all the same colour, or covering them in similar fabrics, helps enormously. Another good trick is to distract the eye in some way; paint the walls of a room in a punchy colour, to divert attention away from mismatching furniture.

SIMPLE HARMONIES

In a first home, your priorities are to make the most of what you've got, and to furnish your home with an eye to the future. Here, striped fabrics are used to create a visual link between a living and a dining area, and to cover up worn or makeshift furniture. Sturdy shelves and baskets provide cheap yet efficient storage, but the dresser in the background is cost-effective in its own way, as it can be used and enjoyed for several years.

USING AND ALLOCATING SPACE

Before you begin to think about re-decorating your home, look closely at how you and your family use it. Your lifestyle may have changed in recent years: one or more members of the household may now have decided to work from home, and older children could be spreading out their belongings into every room. If your layout and furnishings cannot cope any more, and what was once a cosy living and dining area is bursting at the seams with toys and computer equipment, no-one will enjoy spending time there. In fact, the focus of family life could well have shifted elsewhere already.

Although it sounds drastic, changing the layout of your home is sometimes the only way to get more out of it. This may mean moving or removing walls, enlarging openings such as doors and windows, creating changes in level, adding an extension or venturing into hitherto under-used spaces, such as attics and basements. It is often disruptive, but it need not be cripplingly expensive, as long as the changes are not structural.

On balance, it may make more sense to reorganize rather than remodel your home. This is surprisingly easy, as long as it doesn't involve moving water pipes and other services. For example, you might give two children a larger shared space, rather than a room each. This would give them space to play. The extra room could be used for other purposes. As rooms above ground level are usually quiet, we automatically turn them into bedrooms. But they are also brighter, and in a built-up area, they catch the sun for longer. Is it not then more sensible to turn one into a home office or living room?

Ask yourself whether you are overloading some rooms by adhering to convention: for example, do you really need to store clothes in the bedroom, or can a dressing area be squeezed onto an adjacent landing? This would not only create a more pleasant sleeping space, but could give you enough room for a home office or exercise area.

HIGH IDEALS *above*

In homes with high ceilings, much of the wasted space is found above your head. Creating a sleeping platform, with workspace underneath, allows several activities to take place within the same area, and can help to make a tall room seem cosier.

VITAL LINKS *right*

It's not just the size of a space that matters: quality is important too. Here, a corridor is treated with as much care as the rooms at each end, and the net result is that every part of the house feels more welcoming, and larger.

THE HEALTHY HOME

NATURAL COLOUR *above*

While natural materials such as wood are often attractive enough to be left bare, applied colour and pattern add charm, especially in simply-furnished spaces like this hallway. The pigments in natural paints are often plant-based, and create a wide variety of subtle colours.

EASTERN THERAPY *right*

Traditional Japanese interiors are a rich source of ideas for anyone looking to create a healthy and peaceful home. Here, a futon, tatami mats, and light-diffusing paper lanterns and blinds help to interpret the look in a Western bedroom.

Follow a few basic principles of healthy home design: use natural materials wherever possible, but try to ensure that they come from sustainable sources; arrange and furnish your home to make the most of natural light; save energy by insulating your home; use energy-efficient appliances, heating and lighting, and run your car as little as possible; keep dust, chemicals and other allergens to a minimum; and avoid waste – recycle and re-use wherever possible.

It is increasingly easy to purchase attractive and ecologically-friendly furniture. It is usually made from wood, which is a renewable resource less likely to contribute to the greenhouse effect. Fast-growing softwoods such as pine and spruce are the most commonly found, followed by temperate hardwoods, such as beech and oak.

The choice of eco-friendly furnishing fabrics is not as wide, but matters are improving steadily: look for cotton that is grown without the use of pesticides and processed without bleaching; and linen, jute, silk and wool. Avoid fabrics which boast an 'easy-care' finish on their labels. This means they have been treated with formaldehyde, a suspected carcinogen. And you may want to check whether any dyes used are based on natural or synthetic substances. Think also about the ways in which you use fabrics: a simple window treatment gathers less dust, and obviously uses less in the way of raw materials, than elaborately swagged and tailed curtains.

Simply dressed windows also allow natural light to penetrate more easily, and so reduce your dependence on artificial lighting. Other ways to harness natural light include: creating reflective surfaces outside your windows, perhaps with the help of pale-coloured paint or paving, or a pond; keeping large items of furniture away from the windows, and bouncing light further into the room with neutral furnishings.

'Green' decorating materials include natural paints, which comprise raw materials such as linseed oil, tree resins, chalk and citrus fruits.

By way of contrast, synthetic paints contain, amongst other things, petrochemicals and plastics, all of which can emit harmful fumes.

As an alternative to painting the walls, you might consider using wallcoverings made from recycled paper, jute or hessian. Furniture can also be finished and coloured with varnishes made from beeswax and shellac, or stains made from plant extracts or minerals and dispersed in natural binders.

Reducing the number of toxic chemicals in your home also means paying close attention to the detergents, polishes, fresheners and toiletries you use. The average kitchen and bathroom contains an enormous and bewildering array of chemicals, including formaldehyde, phosphates, phenols, ketones, ammonia and chlorine. All of these are known to be environmental pollutants, and highly irritant or poisonous if swallowed. Exercise care in how you use, store and dispose of household products, and choose biodegradable and phosphate-free cleaners wherever possible.

Better still, make your own healthy and low-cost alternatives. Try using borax as a scouring powder and stain remover; lemon juice for descaling kettles and shower heads; white vinegar as a disinfectant; beeswax for polishing furniture; and a few drops of an essential oil burned in a vaporizer as an air freshener.

Finally, think about ways of creating less waste: don't buy goods which are over-packaged – choose those which come in re-usable packaging, such as glass storage jars and bottles, instead. Re-use materials such as paper, wood and textiles wherever possible. And recycle the waste that cannot easily be re-used: glass, paper, cans, some plastics, textiles, organic waste and building materials are all recyclable, as long as you separate them from one another.

Remember also to dispose of hazardous waste safely. Batteries of all types, many household chemicals, medicines, paints and solvents should be taken to waste collection centres.

SIMPLY SCANDINAVIAN

WHITE LIGHT

Mixing old and new comes naturally to Scandinavian homeowners. In an all-white dining room, 1950s 'Butterfly' chairs by the Danish designer Arne Jacobsen, *left*, look perfectly at home in a room lined with traditional tongue-and-groove panelling.

The challenge faced by many households today is how to accommodate ever-increasing quantities of home entertainment equipment and other personal possessions, without losing sight of the need for simply-furnished and comfortable surroundings *right*.

Since the 18th century, Swedish homes have been characterized by a love of light, simplicity and natural materials. Severe weather conditions and forest-covered landscapes made life hard for the majority of people until industrialization in the mid-19th century. Homes were filled with plain or simply decorated surfaces, yet the result was far from austere.

Good design was, and still is, seen as a way of improving living standards for all. Products were easy to use and care for, hygienic, good to look at, and widely available. Artists were employed by factories to design china, glassware and other household objects. And while, during the 1920s and 1930s the Bauhaus movement's machine-made aesthetic, with its use of glass and steel, held sway in much of Europe and America, many prominent Scandinavian archi-

tects continued to advocate the use of natural materials such as wood, to create furniture with expressive lines and character. Hard, rectilinear shapes were felt to go against the natural law.

When the first Ikea showroom was opened in the 1950s in the small town of Älmhult in southern Sweden by Ingvar Kamprad (the I and K in the company's name are his initials, the E stands for Elmtaryd, the farm he grew up on, and A is for the local village of Agunnaryd), it too set out, in his words, to: "offer a wide range of home furnishing items of good design and function, at prices so low, that the majority of people can afford to buy them." With its unique product range, much of it flat-packed for self-assembly and easy transportation, it soon became the largest and most influential home furnishings retailer in Sweden.

CHAPTER ONE

LIVING SPACES

Living spaces are changing. While they once exuded a stiff, formal air, these days they often double up as playrooms, home entertainment areas and hobbies spaces.

Exploit the new informality by creating a flexible furniture layout; modular storage can be rearranged as your needs change, and furniture on castors makes a change of style and atmosphere both possible and appealing. Accessories play a central role, as they can be updated or moved around to suit the seasons or your mood.

This chapter shows suggested furniture layouts for different-shaped rooms, tells you how to set a style and offers advice on focal points, colour and simple window treatments.

EASY LIVING

The days when a living room was reserved only for formal or special occasions, and decorating it was a matter of following rigid sets of rules, are long gone. Today's relaxed attitude to living and entertaining means that anything goes.

The ideal living space should be smart yet informal, functional but elegant, and a pleasure to use, whether you are alone or surrounded by family and friends. It should be capable of accommodating activities as diverse as children playing or adapting a sofa-bed for putting up overnight guests. In fact it has to be one of the most flexible rooms in the house.

When you begin to design a living room from scratch, there is much to consider. Making yourself comfortable is not simply a matter of finding the right chairs. Although seating is important, other considerations merit special attention. You need to provide the right levels of warmth and light, give yourself room to move around the furniture, create a sense of calm and enclosure, and surround yourself with things that you know and cherish.

A successful and functional living room should offer a solution to the problem of long-term storage or display space for items such as books and tableware, as well as allowing you to keep temporary clutter from work or hobbies firmly in check. Ideally, the layout of the room should allow different members of the household to read, watch television and listen to music – all at the same time, if need be.

Designing a cosy and practical living space takes time and planning, but in the following pages you will find plenty of tried and trusted solutions to make it easier for you.

NATURAL FAVOURITES

Mixing rather than matching is the key to creating a stylish and welcoming room. Choose furnishings because you like them, not simply because they 'go' with each other. These natural materials in neutral shades show a particular affinity for one another because of their complementary textures.

PLACING FURNITURE

When planning your furniture layout, respect the existing proportions of the space. Using the shape and character of the room as your starting point, consider such factors as the height of the ceiling; the location of the fireplace, if there is one; and the size and position of the windows. These elements will often suggest possible furniture shapes and layouts.

If you view the space and its contents as a whole, rather than an area into which you will place a collection of objects, each element will look as if it is really meant to be there.

A successful living room should contain the colours, textures and decorative styles which you find especially appealing. Inspiration can come from books, magazines, other people's homes, a scrap of fabric, or perhaps a combination of all these. The important thing is not the source itself, but how you use it to plan or refine a look. The most stylish and successful rooms are not those which slavishly follow a theme, but those which evolve gradually.

SOCIAL CIRCLE *above*

When you group armchairs and sofas around a low table, allow plenty of room for outstretched feet but avoid placing chairs so far apart that the seating area loses its sense of intimacy.

OPEN PLAN *right*

Flexibility is an important part of space planning, because the way you use a room changes regularly. The appeal of this armchair on wheels, adjustable shelving and lightweight occasional furniture is due to their versatility.

SPACE PLANNING

All living spaces, whatever their shape or size, serve the same basic purposes; this is where we sit and relax, store or display certain types of possessions, and spend at least some of our leisure time being entertained by the television, computer games and hi-fi systems. Sometimes, we eat and socialize in here too.

Comfortable seating in a living room is a must. It can take the form of sofas, armchairs, ottomans or footstools, day-beds or *chaises longues* – even a simple pile of cushions if the mood strikes you. Any seating you choose should support your back and be comfortable for reasonable lengths of time, and be grouped in a way that makes it easy to be both solitary and sociable. A single sofa is perfectly adequate if you are alone for much of the time, but a touch awkward if there are two of you.

If space permits, another sofa could be the answer. Two sofas directly facing each other can look a little too formal, but positioning them at an angle to each other will make for a more friendly atmosphere.

Furniture should be arranged so as not to impede your view of focal points such as windows and fireplaces. Grouping all the seats in a room around the television can make the space seem soulless, especially if not everyone wants

SOFT MODERN

All homes should have at least one room which is an oasis of order and calm. The living room is an obvious contender, but it needs to be filled with furnishings that are functional, comfortable and good to look at. Personalizing the space with favourite objects and pictures matters too.

to watch the television while it is switched on.

Most of us also need plenty of shelving and cupboards, not only in order to keep collections of books, compact discs, glasses and drinks in some sort of order, but also to display and enjoy our favourite possessions.

Finding a blank patch of wall for a cupboard or some shelving is not always easy – fixed features such as doors and radiators have a habit of getting in the way, and few of us can afford custom-built storage. Sometimes, free-standing storage units can double up as room dividers, while low, modular storage systems are designed to slip unobtrusively into corners.

Your surroundings should be flexible enough to change with shifting needs and tastes. Before you rush to base your living room scheme on a quirky, amusing picture or a lurid fabric design, stop and ask yourself whether they will both seem as entertaining and eye-catching in a year's time, or merely tiresome. Similarly, the curtainless windows which flood a room with light on spring mornings will make you feel uneasily exposed on winter evenings, so some form of simple covering is essential to cater for seasonal variations. Good solutions include sheer drapes, wooden slatted blinds and simple roman or roller blinds.

CLASSIC STRIPES

Traditional furniture looks far from stuffy when it's dressed down with paint-effect walls, simple striped fabric and an assortment of colourful cushions. Light flooding in through the undressed windows is subtly filtered by painted window-frames, and greenery is used to bring the outdoors in.

LAYOUT SOLUTIONS

Turning ideas into reality always begins with making a scale plan of your room. This gives you a useful map of the area, allows you to plan your decorative campaign and helps to highlight any potential blackspots or awkward corners. It allows you to look at your home as a professional might; that is, objectively. Making a plan of the room will reveal its true shape and save you from having to guess whether an item of furniture will fit into the space.

To make a plan you will need: a sharp pencil; a retractable steel or fibreglass tape measure or an extendable rule (sewing tape-measures are too short and they can stretch); a ruler; graph paper with either metric or imperial divisions – stick to one or the other; and a calculator.

Begin by making a rough sketch of the floor area, and mark in the position of the doors, windows, fireplaces, alcoves and fixed features such as radiators and built-in cupboards.

Next, decide on a scale for your measured drawing. This enables you to reproduce your room in miniature. You might, for example, decide that each metre (inch) should be represented by 5cm (2in) on the graph paper, or use 1.25cm (½in) to indicate 30cm (12in). Use the same scale for all parts of the drawing.

Now, measure each section of wall, each opening, and all the features, one at a time, and mark them to scale on your graph paper in the correct positions. Work as accurately as possible, and if a wall has an opening, recess or some other feature, double check your measurements by taking both the individual and overall dimensions. Also, measure the room from corner to corner, and see whether these figures correspond to those on your plan. They may not, because the corners of rooms are not always set at right angles. The drawing may have to be altered slightly to take account of this fact. Once you are happy with the plan, make several photocopies. Either sketch possible furniture arrangements on each sheet, or cut out furniture shapes in card.

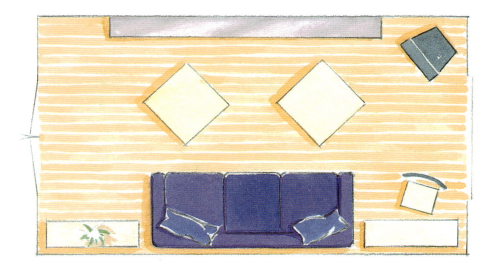

SMALL AND NARROW ROOMS

A sofa and two square ottomans provide flexible seating, while high side tables can be used for both display and work. On the opposite wall, a long run of low shelving visually balances the sofa.

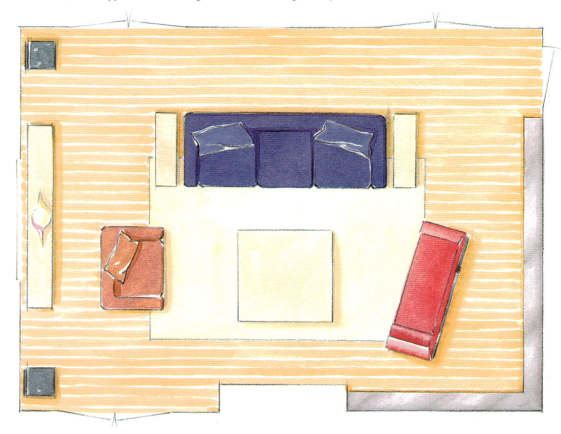

AWKWARDLY-SHAPED ROOMS

Pulling furniture away from the walls improves circulation in rooms with lots of doors. To create a feeling of cosiness, the seating is grouped around a rug, while storage units are arranged in one corner.

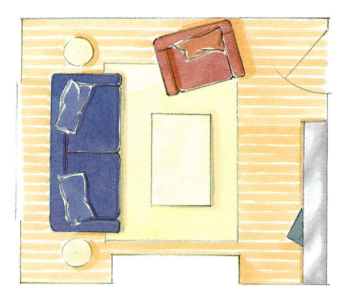

SMALL ROOMS

Placing the sofa as far away from the door as possible helps to reduce its impact as you enter the room. The floor is kept clear to maximize the sense of space.

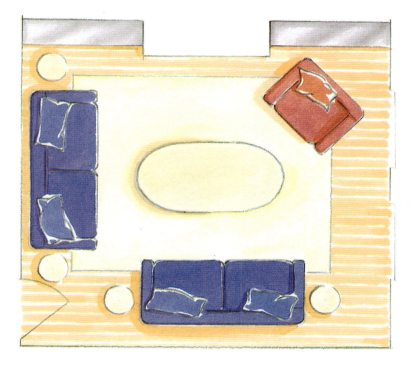

BOXY ROOMS

Using the alcoves for storage helps to improve the proportions of a boxy room. Two sofas and an armchair allow for a variety of seating arrangements.

WORKING TO A BUDGET

- No home-decorating task, however large or small, is as cheap as you first think. Calculate how much you want to spend and add roughly 20 per cent as a contingency.

- Make sure you get the basics right first; these include heating, electrical wiring, structural elements and flooring. You may have to hire the services of professionals such as architects and electricians. Have you included these costs in your calculations?

- Think about whether you can re-use existing furniture and fittings. Can any of them be renovated or updated in some way?

- If you cannot afford to do anything about battered fixtures such as built-in furniture, paint them the same colour as their surroundings.

- In a living room, your furnishing priorities should include comfortable and supportive seating and lighting that allows you to change the mood of the room.

- Inexpensive cotton rugs or dhurries add instant character to a room. They divert attention away from the edges of the living space — useful if you have less than perfect walls, or a motley collection of furniture.

- Cover up worn-looking upholstered furniture with draped sheets, blankets or throws.

- The cheapest and fastest way to freshen up a room and its contents is to apply a coat of paint. Use it to lend unity to a disparate group of objects, and to add character, perhaps in the form of applied pattern and texture.

MIXED BUNCH

A range of chair types allows you to adapt a room to different purposes. Decorative order is maintained by covering them in neutral fabrics.

PREPARING FOR WORK

Unless you are moving into a completely bare shell, the first stage of any decorating job is the 'making ready'. Remove all the furniture and furnishings, or at any rate those items that can be carried easily; the rest can be moved into the centre of the room and covered with dust-sheets, secured with parcel or masking tape. Floor-coverings and built-in furniture can also be protected in this way. Take down curtain tracks or poles and light fittings. If you have a chimney, it is worth having it swept at this stage.

If you plan to make structural changes to the space – by moving the door perhaps, or knocking through into an adjacent room, do this next. Some of these jobs can only be carried out with official permission from your local government or building authority. This can take time, and must be obtained before you begin work, so plan well ahead and consult a professional architect or surveyor if necessary.

Making simple alterations to the fabric of a room can have dramatic results. Moving a door, or even changing the direction in which it opens, can make it easier to create a comfortable furniture layout or bring extra light into the room. Taking down a wall, or creating an opening within it, will create new and interesting vistas. Partition walls can be used to break up a room into several smaller areas, or to create alcoves for shelving. Dividing walls can also be built to half-height, so as not to screen off the room completely.

Think carefully about structural changes. The end result should have graceful proportions and be easy to move around in. It should also be sensitive to the existing architecture; avoid placing partitions against, or directly in front of, features such as windows or fireplaces.

There are, of course, less drastic ways to alter a room's architectural character. It is easy to bring featureless walls to life by fixing on simple panelling made from lengths of softwood or medium-density fibreboard in a regular grid pattern – it looks surprisingly smart. Create a more rustic look with tongue-and-groove boarding, which is also a good quick fix for badly damaged internal walls. It may be possible to add a fixed feature such as a wood-burning stove – an efficient source of heat, and a stylish focal point. These stoves should always be fitted by a specialist, as their use is governed by stringent installation and maintenance rules.

Modern water-based paints and heavyweight wallpapers make it easier than ever to achieve good results, but a certain amount of preparation is necessary, and advisable, as it gives a more professional, longer-lasting finish. Depending on the condition of the existing surfaces in your room, your basic 'making ready' jobs are listed right.

START LINE

Emptying a room of its contents can often help you to see it in a new light. You get a better idea of its true size and the kind of light that comes into the room – both of which can spark off ideas.

MAKING READY

- Strip paper from the walls and ceiling. Wash the surfaces to remove the old size and paste, then sand them to provide a key for the new finish.

- Repair and fill small holes and cracks in the plaster or plasterboard.

- Scrape or chemically strip old paint and varnish from the wood and metalwork, then fill any cracks, sand down the surfaces and prime them for repainting.

- It is often easier to have doors and shutters stripped professionally. However, if you prefer to do it yourself, first take them off their hinges and place them on a flat surface, such as an old table or trestle, before stripping.

- Finally, wash all the surfaces with warm water and a little liquid household detergent, starting with the ceiling and working downwards. Leave these to dry before decorating.

WORKING SAFELY

- Always store tools and equipment under lock and key. Keep chemicals, cleaners and paint in clearly labelled containers, and lock them away, out of the reach of children.

- When using a ladder, check that all rungs are fixed securely and that it is large enough for the job. If the ladder extends, leave at least three rungs overlapping in the centre. Check that both legs of the stepladder stand squarely on the ground and are locked into position. Do not balance paint or tools on the rungs; use a ladder, hook or shelf instead.

- Always work in a well-lit and ventilated area, and try to clear up as you go along.

- Do not operate power tools and blow torches unless you understand how to use them. Follow the manufacturers' instructions when you need to refresh the power source, or change a blade or drill bit.

- When using cutting tools, try to cut away from the body, and keep your fingers behind the blade at all times.

- Wear the right protective clothing and eyeshields for the job.

- Do not try to do too much at once – it is the surest way to make mistakes.

SOURCES OF INSPIRATION

How do you choose a decorative style for your living room? Is it a case of leafing through piles of books and magazines to see if there might be one picture that resembles your own home? Do you have to be historically faithful to the building or neighbourhood? Is it really true that a scrap of fabric or picture postcard contains enough information to enable you to decorate the whole room?

The answer is that none of these approaches, on their own, will help you find the look that suits you. For that, you first have to ask a few questions: 'what do I want from this room? Do I want it to be lively yet cosy, or filled with light and space? Is it a daytime or a night-time room? Does the current decor make me feel bored, or jumpy? Is it too cool, or too stuffy?'

The idea is to build up a picture of the atmosphere that you would like to create; to think about rooms which have made you feel especially happy or comfortable – if you like, to daydream a little.

You might, for example, have fond memories of a place where you spent childhood holidays, or always feel drawn towards a certain type of home when you browse through magazines. There is no point in trying to recreate these rooms down to the finest detail – it would be impossible; but there are always elements that you can adapt. If you happen to love quarry tiled floors, but laying one in your apartment is not an option, why not incorporate the idea in the form of varnished terracotta plant holders? or a smart red and white chequerboard rug?

Converting a vague sense of what you would like into a three-dimensional living room can seem like an impossible task, but it is much easier if you collect all the images that inspire you, along with possible colour or materials samples, in one place. Fix them onto a sheet of paper or board, and view them in the room that you are planning to change. Do this more than once over a period of several days, so that you get an idea of how the room might look on sunny or overcast days, as well as at night. You will gradually begin to see how the various elements work together – whether or not they go with each other – and get a better idea of where changes are called for.

Playing with colour, pattern and texture is one of the most enjoyable aspects of decorat-

PLAN OF LIVING ROOM

Treat lighting as a vital part of the design, not as an afterthought, and make the best use of natural light.

Seating can be placed in the centre of the room as well as around the edges.

Provide surfaces near chairs on which to rest a cup or newspaper.

ing, but too often the fear of making mistakes tempts us to settle for the safest option in the hope that it will offend no-one, and be easy to live with. This is a mistake, as you are much more likely to enjoy being in a room that makes a positive statement than being in one which makes little or no impression.

For example, if you hanker after an all-white room, do not settle for brilliant white walls and one or two pale pieces of furniture. The appeal of this sort of room lies in textural contrasts, so mix frosted glass with smooth china and carved wood, or fine linen with lace and old stone.

You have to be very sure of yourself to adopt an all-or-nothing approach with strong colour and bold pattern. However, you can add colour gradually to the scheme, until you arrive at a level of saturation with which you feel comfortable. If you think that your room needs a shot of lime green, add a small amount in the form of a pair of vases or cushions to gauge the effect, then you can decide whether to buy a new rug or repaint the walls in your chosen shade. Mixtures of colour and pattern can be unpredictable, but decorating is no fun without an element of surprise.

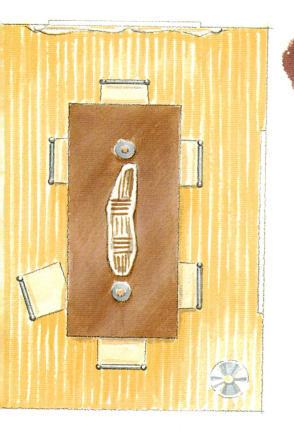

A bold wall colour can dramatically alter the mood at one end of the room.

A table in an eating area can double up as a temporary workspace when needed.

Freestanding shelving units act as room dividers or screens, as well as providing storage.

COMBINING COLOURS

- Create a harmonious scheme by using two or three shades of the same colour, or different colours which are closely related in tone, such as white, pale grey and stone.

- A vibrant or contrasting scheme consists of colours which complement each other, such as blue and orange or scarlet red and green. They are rarely used in equal quantities; instead, one is used as an accent, or as a softer shade. An intermediary or neutral colour is often added to calm things down.

- Monochromatic colour schemes are restful, but small amounts of accent colour need to be added to stop them looking lifeless. The amount of colour you add needs to be finely judged; you know there is not enough of a colour when it looks lost, and you have added too much when it becomes a distraction.

- Different colours can be applied in layers over one another in the form of paint effects on walls and a number of transparent fabrics over a window. Colour layering is softer than one flat tone and is a good source of texture in a room.

- A lifeless colour scheme can often be resuscitated by making one of the shades very slightly lighter or slightly darker.

PAINT SELECTION

To get a better idea of how colours work in *situ*, first paint a small area of wall, preferably near a corner. Look at the colours in different lights, over several days. Place furniture nearby to give you an impression of what the end result might look like.

REFINING THE LOOK

PLAYING WITH SCALE

A rectangular picture *left* is balanced visually by the loose grouping of smaller objects. A cube-shaped vase *below* is a neat setting for a spreading flower arrangement while the cupboard doors *bottom* conceal a home entertainment centre. Generous armchairs *right* are enlivened with spotty cushions.

The walls are decorated and the main items of furniture are in position; now comes the fun part. Professionals call it styling, but a more accurate description of the process would be 'refining the look'. This is when you set about creating the right atmosphere in a room: by mixing old and new perhaps, or rustic and modern; and by experimenting with colour, pattern, texture and scale. Any swatches, postcards or magazine pages that you have collected really come into their own at this point. Use them as a starting point for your ideas. One might suggest a possible mantelpiece arrangement for example, while another might give you the right shade of blue for the cushions.

Professional decorators bring each part of a room to life by treating it as an exercise in contrasts. A plain, thick shelf is used to display ornately carved figures, for example, or the shape of a curvy armchair might be emphasized by placing it next to a simple side table.

Playing elements of a room against one another in this way can help to create a feeling of spaciousness. In the room shown here and on the previous page, the fireplace and painted cupboard balance one another in terms of size, so the overall effect is less overpowering than if either had been used alone. Also, placing the dining furniture near a wall of a similar colour distances it from the rest of the room.

PAINTED CUPBOARD

Decorative furniture painting has a long and varied history in many parts of the world, especially in North America and Europe. Recently, painted furniture and the traditional water-based paints used for it have become popular once again, with the emphasis on eco-friendly decoration.

The great attraction of painted furniture is that you can age or 'distress' a new, cheap piece of pine furniture to make it look like a valued family heirloom. Equally, battered old pieces can be rejuvenated and improved by the addition of several layers of water-based paint, sanded back to reveal the grain between each application. The result is a gently aged effect.

If you start off with untreated wooden furniture, then you need only prepare the surface by sanding it smooth. However, if you have a heavily painted or stained piece, strip away the old layers of paint or unwanted varnish until you get back to the natural grain and the surface is smooth. Use industrial-grade sandpaper, wire wool or, if there are many layers of paint to remove, an electric paint stripper.

The old armoire cupboard shown here was already stripped of existing paint so it needed no preparation other than rubbing with candle wax to start off the 'ageing' process. Candle-wax automatically gives an instant and credible 'aged' effect – the greater the area that has wax applied to it, the more 'distressed' the result.

MATERIALS

One large candle

Water-based paint in three colours – light burgundy, dark burgundy and cream

Three paintbrushes, one 12mm (½ in), two 5cm (2in)

Wire wool

Water-based natural or tinted finishing wax (optional)

A soft rag for polishing

1 PREPARING THE SURFACE

Rub candle-wax on to all the areas you want the bare wood to show through. This produces a barrier through which the paint does not penetrate. For an authentic look, choose areas where natural wearing would occur, such as corners, edges and mouldings. For a heavily distressed effect, rub the flat panels too.

2 APPLYING COLOUR

Apply cream paint to flat centre panels, using the 5cm (2in) brush. The edging does not have to be too precise as you will ultimately use wire wool to 'distress' it. Next, apply the light burgundy to the highlighted area, using another 5cm (2in) paintbrush. Finally, apply dark burgundy to fill in details at edgings and mouldings.

3 SURFACE-AGEING

Once the painted wood is completely dry, rub the surface with wire wool to remove the layers of paint and the wax in a haphazard manner. This will reveal the wooden surface below and create a milky sheen, lightening the colour considerably. Finish off, if desired, by applying a coat of wax and buffing it up with a soft cloth.

INSTANT WINDOW TREATMENTS

It makes aesthetic as well as economic sense to use quick and easy window treatments. For one thing, most of us love walking into rooms filled with daylight. And a simple drape or flourish of fabric at a window often makes a better contrast to bulky furniture than formal curtains.

The fastest way to dress a window is to drape a length or two of fabric over a pole. In general, the fabric should be a little more than twice as long as the distance from the pole to the floor, so that each end reaches the floor when it is in place. If a lightweight fabric is used, it will be necessary to secure or weight it to prevent it from sliding onto the floor.

Lengths of fabric can be stapled or pinned to a window frame too. As these are difficult to draw, they are best suited to those occasions when you need to shut out the view. A less drastic option, which is also easier to clean, is to fix pegs or rings near the top of the window frame, and suspend panels of fabric between them by knotting the corners.

If you like the neat finish that a curtain pole gives, but are worried about choosing, and paying for, a proper curtain heading, then curtain clips may be the answer. These can be threaded onto a pole just like curtain rings, but they are attached to the fabric like clothes pegs, so there's no need for sewing, or working out where to put the hook in a heading tape.

SHEER ELEGANCE *left*

Lightweight, semi-transparent fabrics make wonderful instant curtains, but weight them in some way so that they hang better. Here, panels of contrasting fabric are used to create a deep edging.

DRAPED FABRIC *right*

IKEA 'Omkret' drape hooks can be used to create a tiny swag of fabric at the top of the window, or to fashion asymmetrical Empire-style drapes, as here. The fabric is caught just above window-sill height with a short length of ribbon slipped over a concealed hook.

1 MAKING A GATHER

Fix one Omkret to either side of the window frame. Bunch up your fabric, leaving enough slack to fall in a fold on the floor. Gather a generous section of fabric at the top of the window and place over the Omkret.

2 LOOPING THE FABRIC

Take a short section of the fabric from below the Omkret and feed it through the metal spiral from behind, to form a small loop.

3 CREATING A SWAG

Place the fabric loop over the end of the spiral and open out the fabric folds slightly at either side to conceal the Omkret from view.

4 ASYMMETRIC GLAMOUR

Repeat on the other side of the window. Make sure you use the correct Omkret for each side. A similar window treatment can be acheived using any simple drape hook.

WINDOW DRESSING

It's easy to be frightened by curtains. The permutations can seem endless, improbably large quantities of fabric are often needed, and you may have to live with your mistakes for some time. However, finding the right look becomes much easier if you take the shape and size of the window as a starting point; if they are a stunning architectural feature, or if they frame an inspiring view, cover them up as little as possible. You need not cover them at all if the windows are fitted with shutters, there are no draughts and you are not overlooked.

For most of us, however, the problem is often to find a style that helps to disguise badly proportioned windows. Those that are set too low, or too square for the room, can be made to look more graceful by mounting blinds above the frame, rather than on it – this makes the window look higher. Very narrow examples can be made to look wider by extending the pole, so that drapes hang on either side of the frame.

If the problem seems to be that the windows are too close to the ceiling, hanging curtains so that they dip below sill level can help, as it draws the eye downwards.

Curtains should also complement a room's architectural style. If it has high ceilings and interesting details, it is less likely to be overwhelmed by an elaborate treatment, but will suit the clean lines of a roman or roller blind just as well. In humbler or more modern rooms, it is best to keep it simple. Anything more complicated than a tailored blind, or draw curtains finished at the top with a pole or simple pelmet, starts to look overdone.

Window treatments should be chosen as an integral part of the decor, and not added as an afterthought. Deep folds of plain fabric and simple blinds suit minimally-furnished rooms. In richly decorated rooms, the fabrics used at the window should tie in with the rest of the scheme, but here too, it helps to keep the treatment as unfussy as possible, as this gives the space chance to breathe.

Curtains are not merely practical elements in a room, they add a decorative flourish and impart a sense of luxury. For this reason, never skimp on fabric; always buy the amount required for the style of heading you have chosen. If it looks as though you might exceed your budget, opt for a cheaper fabric instead.

Consider adding a pelmet or valance at the top of a simple window treatment, as this will make it look more impressive, and can be used to hide any ugly track. But ensure that the pelmet is not made too deep, as it can block out a considerable amount of natural light.

CURTAIN HEADINGS *below*

A heading is the style of pleats or gathers used at the top of a curtain. It determines whether the final effect created is skimpy or full, and plays a large part in defining the overall style. Whichever method you use, it should make the curtains easy to draw.

TYPES OF CURTAIN HEADINGS

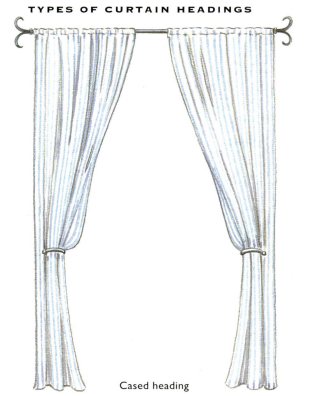

Cased heading

Metal curtain clips

Looped heading

Cartridge pleats

Wooden rings with clips

Eyelet and cord heading

Shirred heading with clips

Threaded fabric heading

Contrasting loops with bows

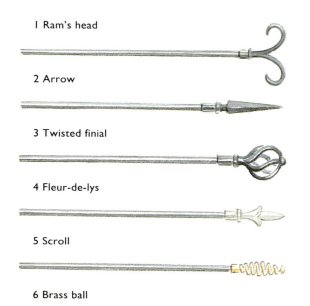

1 Ram's head

2 Arrow

3 Twisted finial

4 Fleur-de-lys

5 Scroll

6 Brass ball

POLES AND FINIALS *left*

Poles take most of the curtain weight, so they tend to be made from rigid materials such as wood and metal. They are usually fixed just above the window frame, but it's worth experimenting a little with their position to see what suits the room best. Finials stop the curtain from sliding off the end of the pole, but their main role is to be decorative, so they are often whimsical in style.

TIE-BACKS AND DRAPE HOOKS *left*

Tie-backs and drape hooks hold curtains away from windows in order to let in natural light. They also help support the weight of heavy curtains and are usually fixed just above sill-height for floor-length curtains but halfway down the window for sill-mounted types.

1 Tie-back
2 Drape hook
3 Fabric holder
4 Fabric clip
5 Tie-back
6 Drape hook
7 Fabric clip
8 Curtain clip

WINDOW DRESSING OPTIONS

- Fabrics fall and drape in different ways, so choose the one which does the job best. Tailored blinds look best in stiffer fabrics such as closely-woven linens or canvas, while curtains that are required to drape should be made from fabrics which create soft folds.

- Controlling the light in a bright room is easier if you create a layered effect with blinds or sheers, and simple draw curtains on top.

- Trimmings help to liven up plain drapes, and they can be used to pick out colours used elsewhere in the room — thereby creating a pulled-together look. Try edging curtains or blinds with a band of contrasting fabric, or tying short lengths of ribbon around individual curtain rings.

- An almost-invisible method of hanging curtains is to suspend them from tensioned steel wire. This needs to run from one wall to another, or inside a window recess.

- If privacy is not an issue, try dressing just the top of the window with a swag of translucent fabric, or a valance made from a gathered or pleated fabric.

- If you plan to use a white or pale-coloured fabric, consider adding a draw rod to the leading edge of the curtain to keep it clean.

- Hang two or three blinds over the width of a large window, instead of a single one. It looks better and makes it easier to control the light level of the room.

PARALLEL LINES

Goblet-pleated floor-length drapes are combined with wooden venetian blinds for a pretty but tailored look.

ARCHITECTURAL FOCAL POINTS

Fireplaces can seem rather lifeless when they're not in use, but this is easily solved by accessorizing them with fire tools or screens, and piles of pebbles or driftwood.

In reality most rooms have more than one focal point: in many cases, it is the windows *far left*. But it could well be a door, a wall, a work of art or the television *left*.

HOT PROPERTIES

All rooms need at least one feature which draws your eyes towards it, an element which emphasizes a style or decorative approach without overwhelming the rest of the room. In the living rooms of many older houses, the fireplace is the focal point: sometimes, it is a single attractive object *right*; at other times a simple frame for the fire, *opposite*, a feature that most of us are instinctively drawn to, even when it's tucked into a corner of the room *far right*.

COLOUR AS A FOCAL POINT

Colour, used creatively, is the easiest and freshest way to give a room character. Whether you live in a modern building that is devoid of architectural detail, or in an older property that needs subtly updating, colour is perhaps the most versatile tool in your decorative repertoire. It is also the most powerful; we assign certain colours to different moods, so our reaction to it is therefore always emotional.

Before a colour can be used to make a decorative statement, you have to be absolutely sure it is the one you want. Buy a sample pot of paint, and use it to cover as large an area of wall as possible. You need to be able to look at it from a distance and at different times of the day.

Next think of the practical things that you want the colour to achieve. In south-facing rooms, which have a tendency to overheat, all but the palest or muted shades of green can help to cool them down.

Other colours have a talent for enhancing natural light and brightening rooms; white is the most commonly used, but the cool grey-blues and greens that came to characterize Sweden's Gustavian period in the eighteenth century also had this quality. When rooms are dull and dingy, use pale, crisp, primrose yellow for a fresh, welcoming look.

Use colour to create smaller areas of interest within the same room. A richly coloured wall or painting can bring a sense of intimacy to a dining area; arranging furniture around a rug helps to define a living area in a multi-purpose room.

One of the best things about using colour as a focal point is that it is inherently flexible. A vibrantly coloured rug can be rolled away if you feel like a change, while a sofa can be quietened down with a neutral throw.

Remember also that combining colours is often about getting the proportions or quantities right. While a touch of contrast refreshes the eye, a heavy-handed approach can leave you with too many areas of colour competing madly for your attention.

PLANE SPEAKING

Two small and potentially awkward features, a fireplace and a high window *left*, have been turned into an abstract composition by setting them into a large expanse of colour. This subtly colours reflected light and enriches the neutral shades of the floor and furniture.

CHECK AND STRIPE

Bold patterns work just as well as solid colours when it comes to attracting attention *left below*. Here, a casual grouping creates a study in black and white. The advantage of such arrangements is that they can be changed easily to create a new look.

RAINBOW ROOM

Like blank canvases, white-painted rooms are a good place to play colours off against each other *right*. All the colours of the rainbow seem to be present in this controlled yet lively arrangement.

LIVING ROOM FLOORING

Living-room floors provide us with a comfortable and attractive surface to walk upon, determine the quality of the room's acoustics, and their colours and textures often suggest a starting point for decorative schemes.

Choosing a flooring material merits careful thought. You will need large quantities of your chosen covering and, while you may be happy to redecorate the room every few years, you are unlikely to change the flooring quite so often. Long-lasting, classic materials such as wood, seagrass, carpet and tile, work best.

The colour and pattern of the floor can help to disguise the room's true proportions. Dark colours and strong patterns cause it to shrink, but this can be a welcome diversion in a boxy space, as long as the flooring is not used wall-to-wall. Light colours and small patterns or plain surfaces make a space feel airier. Laying tiles on the diagonal will push the walls outwards, making a small room feel larger.

If the living room leads directly to an outdoor space, consider a floor that is wipe-clean. If the room doubles as a playroom for young children, you should use a covering which is soft underfoot. As a rule, sound bounces about in rooms with ceramic or stone floors, but is deadened or absorbed by carpets. Wooden floors reflect sound cleanly, and are often the best choice for rooms with hi-fis.

CLEAN AND MODERN *far left*

Laminated woodstrip panels are easy to lay yourself, and this light oak finish provides a warm backdrop to a graphic black and white scheme.

SHABBY CHIC *left*

Old or reclaimed boards rarely lie completely straight, but give a room an irregular charm. Uneven boards can create draughts, so use filler to stop any big gaps.

WARM TERRACOTTA *above*

The rich colour of terracotta tiles makes them a good alternative to wood. They feel warm underfoot, and are easy to keep clean. Reseal them regularly with an oil- or wax-based compound.

MAKING LIGHT WORK

Choosing light fittings for your living space depends to a large extent on personal taste: you may feel most at home in a room filled with flickering candles and deep shadows. Or rows of industrial-style fittings highlighting shiny chrome surfaces, may be more your style.

Lights are much more than decorative accessories – they determine how you use and feel about your room, whenever it is dark or dull outside. They allow you to use the space safely and comfortably, whether you are watching television, reading, chatting to friends, working or simply dozing; they can help to enhance architectural detail and decorative features; they can even alter colours and textures. The

right lighting will make a jumbled mess of a room look mysterious and inviting, while the wrong approach can make a lovingly decorated space feel like a station waiting-room.

Getting it right is simply a matter of building in flexibility. In addition to natural daylight, most rooms need a combination of three basic types of artificial lighting: general or background illumination, provided by pendant lights, uplighters and wall washers, for the times when you are moving around or need a little extra brightness on a dull day; task lighting, from a table or study lamp, to provide more light in those areas where you work, read or pursue hobbies; and decorative lighting, in the form of a chandelier

or candlesticks to complement the centrepiece provided by a special table setting.

It also helps to be able to vary the direction and intensity of light fittings. A directable light, such as an adjustable floor lamp, could be used to light a desk when necessary. When the desk is not in use, the light could be swivelled to shine on a painting above it. Or you might live and work in the same room, and wish to change the lighting from bright and business-like to softly relaxing. Fittings with dimmer switches are ideal for changing light levels.

Deciding where to position the lights is a vital part of planning the space, and is best done with the aid of a floor plan. Some styles of fitting,

such as recessed downlighters, need to be installed before you begin to decorate. Others can be incorporated into the design, along with the main items of furniture. Deciding in advance where you want to position sofas and armchairs, makes it easier to work out where you are going to need extra light for reading or close work. And the furniture layout will suggest where you might safely put sources of background light, such as freestanding uplighters. Compromises may have to be made if there are no power sockets nearby.

The energy efficiency of bulbs also matters. Fluorescent bulbs, and the recently developed compact fluorescent lamps, have the longest life and best efficiency, but they cast an unpleasantly artificial light, cannot be dimmed and usually remind people of institutions such as schools and hospitals.

Low-voltage halogen bulbs are slightly less efficient and can be expensive, but they emit a clear, white light which is much closer to natural daylight than other types of bulbs. These are small bulbs, so they can be easily incorporated into unobtrusive fittings. They can also be dimmed. Tungsten bulbs are the most commonly used of all bulbs, even though they have the shortest lifespan and poorest efficiency of all types. They are cheap, however, and emit a reassuringly warm and familiar yellow glow.

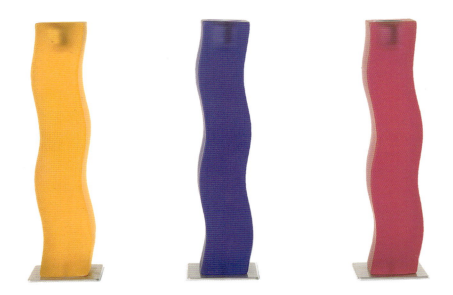

LIVING ROOM LIGHTING

LIGHT SHOW *left*

The domed shade of a table lamp creates a localized pool of light on a display surface, while the tungsten bulb in the fitting enhances the warm tones of the wooden cabinet. Fittings such as this are a good way to draw attention to display areas, but they may not be suitable for focussing on specific objects. For that, a directable light source, such as the wall-mounted low voltage halogen spot, is more suitable. It is used here to illuminate the front panels of the hi-fi system, for easy operation.

Extra areas of brightness need not have a specific purpose, however. They can be used simply to create a more balanced spread of light in the room, or to liven up a dark corner.

QUIET GRACE *below left*

Rooms with a strong architectural character need only the simplest of furnishings. Here, an arching low-voltage floor lamp echoes the shape of a terracotta jar, yet it has the virtue of being almost transparent when set in a vista of angled beams and cut-away partitions.

THE FLEXIBLE APPROACH *right*

Lighting a living space should always be a matter of giving yourself plenty of options. You may not use them all at once, but it's good to know that you have them. Here, a floor lamp and an adjustable arm-style fitting provide light to read by, while pendants hung low over the tables create the right ambience for dining and relaxed conversation.

Decorative objects are lit from above with a variety of sources, including picture lights, surface-mounted downlighters and cabinet fittings. As a rule, picture lights should be angled towards the image to minimize reflections and glare, and it should be possible to adjust the angle, as each type of painted surface reflects light in its own way. Glass and ceramics are best lit from above or from the front to accent their shape, colour and texture.

Meanwhile, flickering candles and night-light lanterns, or perhaps a real fire, give a room a primeval sense of security and calm.

STORAGE AND SHELVING

The type of storage you choose for your living space will radically affect its style and atmosphere. Some types, such as built-in cupboards, have great physical presence and can be used to alter the shape of your room; others, such as bookcases, chests of drawers and modular systems, look more like furniture.

Working out which options are best for you is partly a matter of practicalities. Obviously storage should make the best use of the space available. Everyone needs some storage behind closed doors to hide unlovely clutter, but most people want somewhere to show off favourite possessions, whether they consist of several hundred books or a row of weathered pebbles.

Appearances matter too. Try to imagine how an alcove or other likely spaces would look with different types of storage. An alcove, for example, will 'disappear' if fitted with floor-to-ceiling cupboards. But while properly fitted units can help to give the room a minimal, uncluttered feel, badly-made examples will simply drain it of architectural character, and diminish the floor and ceiling area into the bargain.

Your living space is the one area of the home where it really does pay to buy the best storage or shelving that you can afford. It doesn't have to be a grand design made from expensive materials, but it should be well-finished and in keeping with its surroundings.

ON DISPLAY

Tall glass-door cabinets *above left* are useful for displaying large numbers of books in a dust-free and tidy environment. A wall of open shelving *left* suits lighter, more considered arrangements. All the available space is used, but by painting the shelves the same colour as the wall the impact is reduced in this minimally furnished room.

A NATURAL DRAW

Wooden storage cabinets *right* allow you to organize living-room clutter. These ones complement the natural themes of the surrounding decor and furnishings.

DISPLAYING COLLECTIONS

- Always group similar objects together for decorative impact.

- Try to create contrasts of colour, scale and texture. Rustic baskets can be displayed on metal shelves, clear plastic compact-disc containers look good in brightly coloured boxes or cabinets, and a group of photographs looks less self-conscious when housed in a variety of frames.

- Large collections can be overpowering; try punctuating rows of books with different objects or areas of clear space.

- If items are very small, display them in compartmentalized trays or boxes to give each one a frame.

- So-called 'dead' spaces are often ideal for displaying collections. A corner can be put to good use with the addition of a small wall-mounted cupboard or shelf. Narrow areas of wall, such as those found between two windows, are the perfect place to display groups of small pictures. Store fragile items on high shelves to keep them safe.

- Freestanding cabinets or chests will focus your eyes on the lower part of the room; this is a good idea if you have a low ceiling, or if you would prefer to use the space above the units for pictures and lights.

STORED AWAY

The surface of freestanding low cabinets provides a useful area for displaying objects and collections.

Home Entertainment

Whether you watch television a little or a lot, it is as much a part of daily life as sleeping and eating, so deciding where to position the set is an issue that merits careful consideration. A television needs to be clearly visible from nearby seats and should be positioned at a comfortable viewing height – around seated eye level is best. Avoid letting sunlight or bright lights fall across the front of the set.

You may have strong feelings about the extent to which the television makes its presence felt. If you seldom watch television (or wish that you seldom did), or if the room in which it is kept has several uses, there are plenty of good reasons for hiding the set when not in use, including keeping it away from inquisitive children. It can be kept in a cupboard behind doors that close, or on a hydraulic lift that rises out of a cabinet or trunk. Alternatively, putting it on a mobile cart or trolley allows you to wheel it out of sight, or to another part of the room.

On the other hand, in a den or some other room designed around home entertainment equipment, a television is an obvious focal point, and there is no reason why it should not be on permanent view in a corner of the room.

Increasingly, the television does much more than bring you the news or a favourite sitcom. It can be hooked up to the hi-fi, or to the world outside, thanks to home study, shopping and banking facilities. The role played by computers in the home is changing radically too; as well as being a study or leisure tool, they also provide access to a wide range of outside services. The proliferation of new technology has blurred the old dividing lines between work, relaxation and running the household and is bound to affect how we design and use our living spaces in the future.

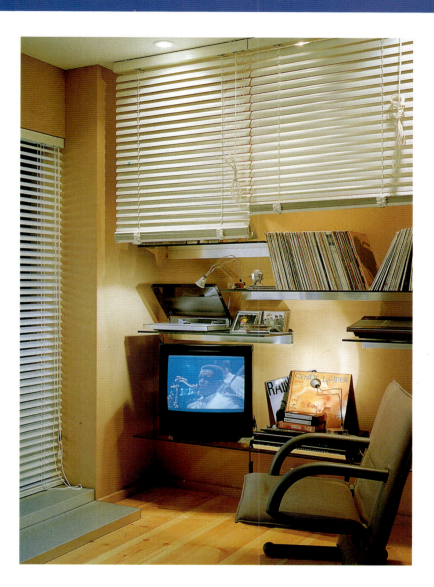

CABLE MANAGEMENT

- A home entertainment centre allows you to link up the television, VCR, hi-fi and computer games equipment with each other. When arranging the components, place the television screen at seated eye level, put the hi-fi above it, and the VCR and games console below so that older children can operate them easily.

- Check that spaces are sufficiently large to house components and still allow room for cables, connectors, plugs and ventilation.

- If the television is set into a cupboard, place it on a carousel and glides. This will allow you to pull the set forward and swivel it for easier viewing.

- Cable and telephone services often need to be used in conjunction with a signal decoder or converter. Place this next to the television for convenience.

- If the number of remote control units in your living space seems to have proliferated, replace them with a 'universal' handset that is capable of operating several items of electrical equipment.

- Keep long lengths of cable neat by looping any slack and securing it with elastic bands or twist-ties.

HOME CINEMA

A night in front of the television becomes a treat when you give yourself the best seat in the house, but remember that sitting too near the television, or too far away, can cause eye strain.

WHERE'S THE TELEVISION? *opposite*

The television should be the focal point of the room only when you want it to be; placing it on a low trolley which can be wheeled out of sight behind a sliding panel is a good way to limit its impact. Mounting the furniture on wheels makes it easier to arrange the room to accommodate several activities.

BLIND FAITH *above*

Chunky shelves and venetian blinds provide a smart, low-cost alternative to built-in storage or freestanding furniture. Short lengths of shelving are less likely to bow when laden with heavy items. Stagger their heights to add visual interest and provide natural support for vertically stacked albums.

FLOWER FEAST

It is hard to think of a style of room where flowers would be unnecessary or out of place. They are, in many ways, the perfect finishing touch for a decorative scheme; a simple bunch of seasonal blooms or a few carefully chosen stems add life and a sense of luxury to any room. Flowers are affordable, unless you insist on buying armfuls of exotica in the depths of winter; and they are endlessly renewable – one week you might choose flowers that either highlight or blend subtly with your colour scheme, while the next week you can use them to create a dramatic counterpoint.

Most importantly, they provide a much-needed link with the natural world. If you have a garden, use it as a source of flowers and foliage by growing enough of your favourite blooms and greenery to keep up a regular supply of colour and texture throughout the year. Flowers are one of the easiest, and most charming, ways to bring the outside in. And you need not worry too much about damaging plants; many flowering species benefit from being cut on a regular basis during the growing season, as this encourages stronger foliage and repeated flower production. In winter, when the garden seems rather bare, it may still be a good source of natural foliage such as dried seedpods and leaves, colourful berries, fallen twigs and evergreens such as ferns and ivy.

Even if you do not have a garden, keeping a regular supply of colour and greenery need not be an extravagance if you buy flowers when they are in season. Opt for exuberance in the spring and summer, when large bunches of flowers are affordable. They will instantly fill a city apartment with a sense of the country. At other times, long-lasting arrangements can be made with dried flowers and vegetation. Big, bold shapes, such as those of corn cobs, hogweed, hydrangeas and thistles, work best in modern, boxy rooms, where their dramatic shapes lend definition to simple decoration.

Another approach is to treat individual flowers as beautiful objects in their own right. A

single parrot tulip placed in the right vase has far greater presence than a bunch of the same flowers crammed unsympathetically into a non-descript container. Similarly, two or three flower-erheads floating in a bowl of water make a compelling sight when viewed from above. A few scattered, small arrangements around a room can look dull and bitty. Far better to group them together on a window-sill or mantelpiece for a glorious show of colour.

It is a good idea to keep a collection of containers in several different shapes and sizes, as nothing makes flowers more unhappy-looking than a vase which is too large or too small, or one with a neck that is too wide or narrow.

Clear glass vases are very versatile, as they will blend happily into a variety of decorative styles. Make sure you remove any leaves below the water level to avoid the water becoming slimy, and change the water regularly — preferably daily — to avoid it turning cloudy.

Bright, zingy glass vases make more of a decorative statement, especially when they are filled with vivid blooms in contrasting colours.

Ceramic and metal containers are a good choice for flowers that do not have especially pretty or interesting stems. Flowers can be evenly distributed in the container by putting in a small amount of large-gauge chicken wire or standard florist's foam.

DISPLAY AND DELICIOUS DETAILS

THE FINAL TOUCHES

A stripped-back decorating approach *above* is reinforced by the use of a frameless picture, skeletal-looking candlesticks and an antique birdcage. An overly bleak look is avoided by piling high the sofa with cushions.

In neutrally-decorated rooms *above right*, a flash of accent colour should be echoed elsewhere to make it look like a

conscious decision rather than an afterthought. Propping pictures casually on a surface, or on the floor, makes them seem less precious.

Sometimes, the simplest furniture arrangements work best *opposite below left*. Books and framed photographs, *opposite below right* humanize a room, and there's no reason why they should be confined to shelves or cupboards. A deep windowsill is the perfect place to display a small group of pictures, as they will catch the light without blocking its path into the room.

Finishing touches may often suggest a decorative theme *left*. The various shades of red in the painting are echoed by the simple sofa cover and cushions and, more subtly, in the tones of the traditional butler's tray table and barleytwist lamp base.

DINING ROOMS

TABLE MATTERS

If you love to entertain, and plan dinner parties as though they were theatrical productions, a room dedicated specifically to the purpose of dining *right* is probably high on your list of priorities. Night-time spaces such as this can be decorated like theatre sets; for dramatic effect, only the dining table is lit, and props, such as the tableware, play a much smaller role than the 'stars', or guests.

The temptation to create a fantasy feel with elaborate soft furnishings can be overwhelming, but stale food odours have a habit of clinging to thick carpets and heavy curtains. Try instead to create a sense of occasion with table settings *above*.

Most dining rooms cannot be reserved solely for formal occasions. They need to adapt quickly for use in the daytime, – easily done if they are decorated in fresh and sunny colours *far right*. A solid, practical table in a sunny room is a fine place to work or concentrate on hobbies, yet can be easily dressed up for parties; just add one smart tablecloth, your favourite china and a vase of freshly-picked flowers.

A storage cabinet is useful in a dining room, not only for keeping tableware and linen close at hand, but also to give the room a sense of purpose.

CHAPTER TWO

KITCHENS

Successful, practical kitchens call for careful and creative planning. Every detail counts, from creating an efficient layout to choosing suitable flooring materials and finishing touches such as door furniture. Contain the clutter within well-organized cabinets, but remember that open wall displays of equipment and accessories are practical as well as aesthetic.

Good kitchen design saves time and energy. It can also create extra space for flexible living and relaxing. A table can be used for eating, children's play, occasional work and paying household bills. An awkward corner may be the ideal spot for a cosy armchair and the television.

Classic layouts, space-saving tips and inspiring photographs of kitchens that work are all here for the taking, so use them to create the room that suits you. Think functional but beautiful.

PERFECT KITCHENS

The kitchen is at the heart of family life. It is not simply where you cook and eat, but also where you might do the laundry, keep an eye on the children and carry out the day-to-day running of your home. And this is where family and friends instinctively gather, even when there is a spacious living room next door.

As well as being a place to work, the perfect kitchen has a symbolic function. We expect this room to warm and nourish us, and we often decorate it in a way that suggests an earlier, more peaceful age.

ROOM TO MOVE *above and right*

Space is the most precious commodity of all in a working kitchen, so make the most of it with a combination of storage and display ideas. Most manufacturers offer a range of cupboard styles and worktop finishes to suit any style.

KITCHEN DESIGN SOLUTIONS

The aim of fitted units, so the theory goes, is to make finding a place for everything a little easier, and to an extent, they do. A kitchen in which the sink, stove and refrigerator are easily to hand, perhaps because they have been arranged to form what professional designers call a 'work triangle', will be less tiring to work in (see pages 72-3 for ideas). And a well-planned, fitted kitchen is certainly easier to keep clean than an ad hoc collection of cabinets and open shelves which allows dirt and grease to collect in inaccessible corners.

Kitchen design is not just about creating a practical working space. Even wall-to-wall appliances in stainless steel will not alter the fact that this is a room in a home, not a scientific laboratory. Creating a comfortable atmosphere matters just as much here as elsewhere. The materials that you choose for the walls, floor and furniture need to be easy on the eye and pleasant to touch, as well as easy to clean. If the kitchen is located in a large, multi-purpose area, these elements should also provide a visual link with the rest of the room. And if you have the space, combine fitted cabinets with freestanding furniture, such as an all-purpose table, chair, light or sofa, to create the impression that this is a room for living in too.

ZONES OF ACTIVITY *above*

Natural materials add warmth to a cool but fresh green and white colour scheme, in which a run of base units separates the dining table from the cooking activity.

MOVEABLE FEAST *right*

Screening is a welcome feature in a kitchen which forms part of a larger living space. Storing equipment and condiments on wheels gives this small kitchen a high degree of flexibility.

SMALL KITCHENS

SMALL IS USEFUL

Lack of space is no bar to efficiency in modern kitchens. A galley-style layout and open shelves *left* ensure that equipment can be used and replaced with the minimum of fuss. Less frequently-used items are stored out of the way, on a shelf above the door.

Simple ideas can make a big impact in small spaces *right*. Here, plain wooden cabinets are teamed with black ceramic tiles, used on both floor and walls, and white paint to create a look that is both striking and practical.

When planning a small kitchen try to avoid thinking of it as a poor substitute for a large one. Small kitchens are just as efficient as more spacious rooms. In fact, many serious cooks prefer to work in a space where excursions between cupboard, sink and stove are kept to a minimum and distractions are few.

A certain amount of lateral thinking will be needed to ensure that all the equipment and storage you require will fit in. Many kitchen appliances are available in a compact or scaled-down version; but do check that they meet your household's needs before you buy.

Creating the impression of space is just as important as good space planning; choosing similar tones for the walls and fitted furniture will make them seem less obtrusive, and a view into another room, perhaps via a doorway or serving area, will make a self-contained, small kitchen feel bigger.

CREATING ROOM TO MOVE

- Fold-down or pull-out counters and tabletops allow you to make flexible use of limited floor space. Choose chairs that either stack or fold away when not in use.

- A butcher's block on wheels provides useful extra workspace and storage for essential equipment such as knives and pans.

- Many sinks can be covered with a shaped chopping board to give you an extra worktop. Similarly, if you are buying a new stove, look for one with a sturdy cover.

- Store items which are used everyday in a space between eye and hip level. This will avoid you having to perform repeated bending and stretching in a confined area.

- When choosing base units, remember that pull-out drawers take up less space than conventional doors when opened. They also enable you to better organize the interior.

- Sliding doors take up virtually no space, but you are unlikely to find them on fitted furniture. However, it may be worth using them to screen off the kitchen in an open-plan room.

- When working in the kitchen, make it a habit to clear up and clean as you go along.

SPACE SAVER
When there is no room for a separate kitchen, a cooking area can fit into a space that is not much bigger than a walk-in wardrobe.

If you are designing your kitchen from scratch, your first question should be: 'Is it in the right place?' If you crave a garden view, or an all-purpose family room, you could consider locating the kitchen in another part of the house. If what you really want is more space, it may be possible to knock through into an adjoining room, or increase the amount of usable floor space by moving a doorway or radiator.

This process does not have to be too expensive – it depends on how your home was built, and whether special equipment or skills are needed to remodel it.

Relocating gas, electricity and water supplies can be costly and disruptive, but it may be that the end result justifies the expense if the process forms a minor part of the overall cost of your work. Do check that adequate provision can be made for drainage and ventilation in any new scheme.

When budgetary restrictions prevent radical changes to an existing space, or if you simply wish to refurbish an existing kitchen, your first step should be to look closely at its layout and storage capacity. Is there enough space for the children to play safely? Does it contain all the appliances you need? Could any of these, such as the freezer or washing machine, be sited elsewhere? Do you find yourself constantly short of work space? If so, try to include a generous run of unbroken countertop between the sink and stove. What does not fit into your storage space? Would full-height wall cabinets improve matters?

Once you have an idea of the possible layout, draw an imaginary line between the stove, the sink and the refrigerator. Then ask yourself: 'Is the distance between any of these points so long that I'm going to spend all my time walking

continued overleaf

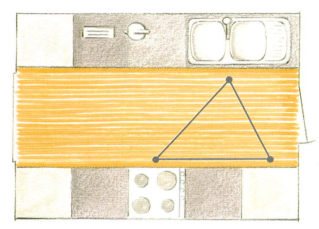

THE GALLEY KITCHEN
A galley kitchen consists of two lines of units at either side of a room. The space between the units should be between 120cm (48in) and 95cm (37in).

THE SINGLE LINE KITCHEN
Best in open-plan and narrow spaces, a single-line kitchen should be planned so that there is as much unbroken worktop space as possible.

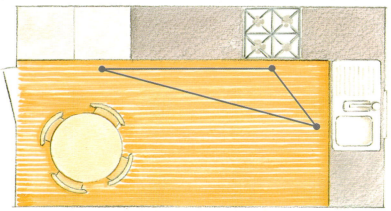

THE L-SHAPED KITCHEN
A good choice if you want to make space for a table. This arrangement is best for narrow rooms where two people want to work simultaneously.

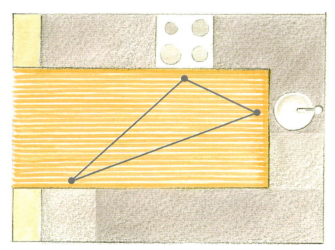

THE U-SHAPED KITCHEN
This gives you large amounts of storage and worktop space, but is only feasible where there are unbroken stretches of wall on three sides of the room.

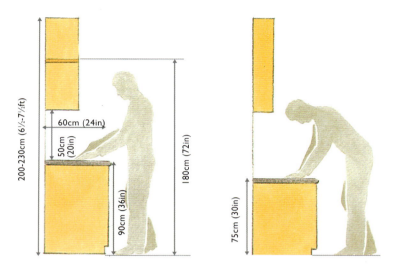

ERGONOMICS

The standard base cupboard height of around 90cm (36in) can be used by most people for light or fiddly cooking tasks. In wall cupboards, shelves up to a height of about 180cm (72in) can be reached easily. Any above this height should store infrequently-used items only.

Heavier tasks such as kneading dough, can be performed more easily at a lower worktop height, say about 75cm (30in).

THE ISLAND KITCHEN

Only large rooms suit this style of layout, as space is required all around the island for working and sitting. If you cook here too, an extractor will be needed.

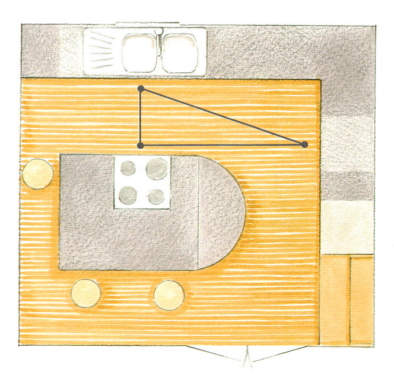

ERGONOMICS

- There should be enough space at each point of the 'work triangle' to allow you to work easily. Make sure that you have somewhere to deposit hot dishes by the oven and stove, and enough space by the sink and refrigerator to rest foodstuffs or a saucepan.

- Try to keep worksurfaces and the floor in and around the 'work triangle' fairly clear, to make working and movement as easy as possible.

- Vary the heights of your worksurfaces. Tasks which require muscle power, such as kneading dough, are best carried out at a slightly lower height than those which require hand-to-eye coordination, such as chopping herbs and vegetables.

- If you are of less than average height, it is easier to look into pans if the stove is set slightly lower than the standard height.

- Too many different worktop heights can make the room look messy. A more practical approach might be to lower a run of units by adjusting the feet behind the base plinth. Or build up the height with a thick cutting board or pastry slab.

- In busy kitchens, site the refrigerator at the end of a run of cabinets; that way, other members of the household can carry out 'raids' without getting in the way of the cook.

TRESTLE ISLAND

A trestle table set in the middle of the room is a practical and affordable alternative to a built-in island unit.

from one to the other? Or so small that the working space is going to feel cramped? Will I find myself bumping into the rest of the household as they pass through the kitchen? Or tripping over guests as they sit at the table?

Identifying where most of the work takes place helps to establish the 'work triangle'. It may not look like a triangle at all. If your kitchen consists of one line of cabinets, then the path will also form a straight line. Forming a work triangle is a very useful way of working out whether your new kitchen will be easy to use. Ideally, the distance between each point of the triangle should measure a little more than a double arm span, roughly 2 metres (6½ feet), although this is rarely the case in real life.

To create a more efficient working area, consider moving one or more points of the triangle to give you longer runs of unbroken worktop. It is often best to leave the sink where it is, as making large-scale plumbing changes is expensive. Changing the position of a cooker or hob is easier, although it should be placed against an exterior wall, for easy ducted extraction.

KITCHEN PLAN

Contemporary and rustic styles of furniture can be successfully combined. Here, melamine-faced units are teamed with solid wood worktops and furniture. Tiling used on both the floor and walls helps to create a unified feel.

A low wall and base cabinets stacked double allow daylight from the balcony to penetrate further into the room.

A freestanding glass-door cabinet gives the food preparation area a cosier feel.

Quarry-tile flooring is non-slip and easy to clean.

Table is placed outside immediate working area.

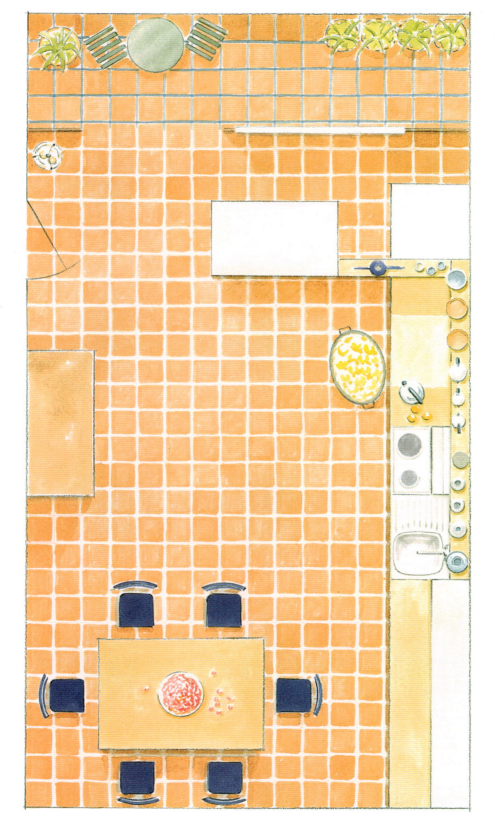

A link with the outdoors is welcome in any kitchen. Continue floor tiling outdoors to create a feeling of space.

Utility area.

Fitting narrow shelves rather than cupboards above the sink and stove creates more headroom.

Stove under base unit.

Separate stove allows you to mix gas and electricity.

Single-drainer sink

Fridge in base unit.

PRACTICALITIES - 1

In theory, a cook could function perfectly in a kitchen with only his or her ingredients, a surface to work on, a water tap, a heat source, a sharp knife and a set of saucepans. Very few do, however. These days, even a basic kitchen contains enough gadgets and appliances to take care of every conceivable chore, which means that choosing the right equipment has never been so time-consuming.

As well as deciding which appliances to buy, and how much money you want to spend, there are questions of maintenance, energy-efficiency and performance to consider. Matters are further complicated by technical jargon, the highly competitive world of electrical appliances retailing, and the fact that newer and better products seem to appear all the time.

One of your first tasks will be to decide whether to build your kitchen around built-in or freestanding appliances. While the former blend into the room's decor more effortlessly and make the room easier to clean, the latter are a great deal cheaper to buy, as you don't need special carcasses and door panels in which to house them.

If you are short of space, look out for dishwashers and refrigerators that can be opened and shut rather like large drawers. They help to alleviate the problems caused by large door swings in tight corners.

Combination appliances, such as microwave oven that can also be used as convection ovens and grills, are another good idea. When used in conjunction with a two-ring stove, this mix provides a flexible and highly space-efficient cooking area in a tiny kitchen. You may also find a combination appliance useful as a second oven if you often feed large numbers of people. It is possible to buy built-in double ovens where one can be used as a microwave, or you may find it easier to install a separate microwave under the stove. Make sure that it is adequately ventilated however. If you only use a microwave for

continued overleaf

SAVING ENERGY AND OTHER RESOURCES

Electrical kitchen appliances are among the biggest consumers of energy in the home. A few items, such as dishwashers and washing machines, can only be used if they are also fed with strong detergents and large amounts of water. The potential for waste is enormous, and it is worth remembering that this depletes not only the earth's resources, but the contents of your wallet too.

Appliance manufacturers are increasingly conscious of environmental hazards and waste, and are striving hard to ensure that their products make much better use of resources than they used to. CFC-free refrigerators and freezers are now the norm. Many dishwashers come equipped with sensors that help to conserve electricity, detergent and water; some new washing machines use only 20 litres (4.4 gallons) of water, a significant advance on the older models which consumed 40 litres (8.8 gallons) per wash. The latest detergents are more concentrated, to cut down on packaging, and less likely to contain non-biodegradable compounds, while some cooking appliances are now made from a light plastic that can be ground down and recycled.

Energy-saving isn't simply a matter of buying the right equipment, however. All appliances should be serviced regularly to maintain their efficiency, and it's worth asking yourself whether you could do the work of some gadgets by hand. Curiously, two of the healthiest cooking techniques also use the least energy; stir-frying and steaming food use limited amounts of fuel, oil and water, and produce delicious results.

COOL BLUE *left*

Freestanding appliances look neater when they are housed under a continuous worktop. However, siting a washing machine next to the cooker is not ideal, as the noise and vibrations emitted by the former do not make for peaceful working conditions in the kitchen.

ALLOCATING CUPBOARD SPACE

- It is difficult to calculate exactly how much storage space you need, not least because the contents of your kitchen change continually. But there are ways of working out what goes where.

- Store saucepans and cooking utensils near the stove or oven. Stack saucepan lids separately to save space.

- Tableware and cutlery should either be stored near the sink and dishwasher so that they can be put away easily, or else near where you eat. To keep them clean, store behind closed doors.

- Store everyday foodstuffs near the food preparation area, perhaps in a pull-out larder. Bulky or heavy items should not be stored too high up or too low down.

- Small amounts of cooking oils, spices and condiments can be kept in airtight containers above the cooker. Avoid storing large quantities, as heat makes them go stale more quickly.

- Try to build one stack of drawers into your design and use it to store cutlery, small gadgets, tea towels, paperwork and other useful odds and ends.

- Pull-out base units are useful for storing baking tins, chopping boards and seldom-used appliances.

- A tall cupboard can be used to store brooms, an ironing board and the vacuum cleaner.

- Always keep medicines and dangerous chemicals in a lockable cabinet, away from heat sources.

STEEL WORKS

Siting a basin on an island unit makes it easier for more than one person to use. Always ensure that the floor nearby has a non-slip surface.

reheating food and cold coffee, it makes more sense to place it near the refrigerator.

A stand-alone microwave should not be built-in above a regular oven, as it may not be designed to withstand extreme heat. Instead, it can be treated like any other small appliance, and either placed on a worktop or fixed to the wall. You may also want to keep other equipment, such as a food processor, coffee grinder, toaster and fruit juicer, close at hand. If so, do check that you have enough worktop space, and a sufficiently large gap between the base and wall cabinets for taller items. There should also be enough power sockets; using multi-plug adaptors and extension cables at worktop level is both unsightly and dangerous.

Choosing the right sinks and taps is also an important task. When space is tight, a large, single sink offers greater flexibility than two small bowls. Other combinations, such as 1½ or 1¾ bowl, may be more suitable for your space, and work habits. Whichever you choose, check that it is roomy enough to take a dirty baking sheet or your largest pan. Taps can be chosen to reflect your own tastes and the style of the kitchen. However, look for a design with a tall spigot, as it will make it easier to fill large pots.

Kitchens suffer more than other rooms when it comes to temperature extremes. Stoves, central-heating boilers and, to a lesser extent, refrigerators and freezers, release heat into the room, but you may still need an extra source of warmth at the very coldest times of year. This will not be a problem if you have underfloor or central heating. Otherwise, try to find space on the wall for a thermostatically controlled electric rail. As well as creating additional heat, it can be used to dry clothes or towels. In summer, a kitchen-full of working appliances can be torture. If you are not lucky enough to have integral air-conditioning or some form of mechanical ventilation system, try to create through draughts by opening windows at each end of the house.

LAUNDRY AND UTILITY AREAS

- While a water- and energy-efficient washing machine is easy to find, few have been designed for quiet operation. Can you cope with the noise in the kitchen, or should it be sited elsewhere?

- To reduce vibration from a washing machine, mount it on a wooden pallet or rubber pads. The former is not suitable if it needs to fit under a countertop.

- Certain kitchen floor materials are better sound-absorbers; timber and cushioned vinyl are quieter than tile, stone and metal.

- Do you need space for drying clothes? Where will the drying rack be stored when it's not in use? A ceiling-mounted drying rack may be a good solution.

- Try to find room for two laundry bags or baskets; one each for clean and dirty clothes.

- Store brooms and mops on special hooks, or else in a tall cupboard with pull-out baskets for storing cleaning supplies.

- Other things to put in a laundry/utility room: shoes on shelves; the boiler; the freezer; and a sink for cleaning mops and shoes. Avoid storing food in here, as it is likely to be both damp and warm.

WASHDAY BLUES

If you have the space for it, a separate laundry area can remove a major source of noise, vibration and condensation from the kitchen.

MATERIALS AND FINISHES

In recent years, there has been a huge increase in the range of materials available for home kitchen use; laminates, solid wood and tiles remain popular, but they are now combined, often in surprising ways, with newcomers such as stainless steel and eco-friendly paints.

Your worktops are where all the action takes place, so they need to be hardwearing and easy to clean, as well as heat-resistant and impervious to food odours and stains.

There is no one material which outperforms the rest in every respect; while solid wood looks warm and ages well, it needs to be oiled regularly and should not be left wet for long periods of time; laminates are economical, easy to clean and available in a wide range of colours and patterns, but they should not be used for cutting on; tiles are resistant to just about everything, except pans of hot fat, but can be expensive when used over a large area.

More unusual worktop materials include: granite, which is heavy and expensive, but it keeps its polished good looks no matter what you do to it; mineral materials such as Corian and Avonite which are easy to shape and highly resistant to burns and marks, but they have to be installed professionally and are therefore expensive; metals such as zinc and stainless steel are hygienic and look stunning when used in sheet form, but require frequent cleaning.

HOT AND COLD *opposite*

Warm wood and coolly efficient stainless steel make spectacular textural contrasts in a sleekly efficient galley kitchen.

PALE TONES *above*

With its connotations of health and simplicity, blond wood and white walls are the classic design solution for many modern kitchens, but they need to be kept immaculately clean and tidy to maintain the effect.

MAKING THE MOST OF WORKTOPS AND CUPBOARDS

- Try to keep worktops clear. Store frequently-used equipment such as knives, or the dish drainer, on wall-mounted racks or shelves. Many small appliances can also be fixed to the walls.

- Worktops should be lit from above to make working easier and safer. Fit fluorescent tubes at the front edge of the undersides of wall cupboards or shelves.

- The undersides of wall cupboards or shelves can be put to better use by adding flip-down shallow drawers, rows of cup-hooks or baskets.

- Laminated cupboard doors can be renovated or customized by sanding the surface, priming it with a suitable undercoat, then rolling or brushing on an oil-based paint. Work in a well-ventilated space.

- Use every inch of cupboard space by installing glass racks, plate stands and other clip-on accessories.

- Fit small interior lights to glass-fronted cabinets.

- Door and drawer handles add a decorative flourish to cabinets, so choose them to complement the style of your room. Consider large and easy-to-grip designs if the kitchen is to be used by older people and children.

COOL KITCHEN

Cabinets and a worktop of different colours combine gracefully with a steel splashback and a wooden floor.

FLOOR AND WALL TREATMENTS

When choosing floor and wall finishes for a kitchen, your deciding factors should be comfort, durability, ease of maintenance, price and eco-friendliness.

For once, the cheapest flooring options are also the easiest to lay, and are amongst the most comfortable. These include linoleum sheet or tile flooring, which is made from natural materials such as linseed oil, cork and hessian. As well as being durable, warm, flexible and available in a wide range of inviting colours, linoleum is easy to fit in awkward corners.

Vinyl flooring, which is often mistakenly called lino, offers many of the same advantages, but is less environmentally friendly, as both the floor and its adhesives give off harmful vapours. Timber and cork floors add texture and subtle colour to a room. They are also hardwearing, warm, comfortable to walk on, and lightweight. They age better than linoleum and vinyl, as long as they are sealed regularly. And they need not be expensive; cork tiles, parquet and tongue-and-groove strip floors are affordable and widely available.

Other practical flooring options include ceramic and stone tiles, which are hardwearing and resistant to most spills and scratches. They can be expensive if used over a large area, and the extra cost isn't easy to justify, as they are also cold, noisy, hard on the feet, difficult to lay well, and perhaps most annoyingly, both hard and fragile at the same time. Terracotta tiles are warmer, and they age beautifully.

Kitchen walls are subject to different kinds of wear and tear; the area behind the stove should be heat- and steam-resistant, and the area behind a worktop, known as a splashback, will need to be impervious to food spills, or oil and water splashes. Ceramic tiles, granite, slate, sheets of metal or toughened glass, and oil-based paints are the most suitable finishes for these areas of the room.

Elsewhere, walls give you the chance to stamp an identity on the room. Wooden panelling can provide noise insulation and has a pleasingly regular texture. It will also conceal imperfections or ugly pipework. Use wallpaper as an easy way to bring colour and pattern into the room; vinyl wallcoverings are the easiest to clean and the most hardwearing.

FLOOR SHOW

below left Chunky open shelving and a terracotta floor are easy to keep clean, and they give this simply furnished kitchen a rustic, wholesome feel.

A sheet vinyl floor in a chequerboard pattern, *below centre*, helps to liven up a scheme that is otherwise restricted to pale and neutral colours.

A wood pattern laminate floor, *below right*, is an affordable luxury if you are equipping and furnishing your kitchen on a tight budget.

Ceramic floor and wall tiles are available in an enormous range of colours, offering limitless possibilities for creating your own style, *right*.

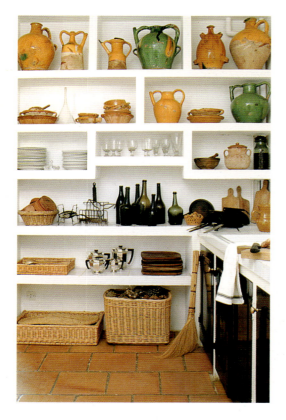

KITCHEN LIGHTING

LIGHT STYLES

Glass-door cabinets above should be fitted with interior lights to allow their contents to be shown off in style. If your kitchen receives plenty of natural daylight, make the most of it by siting worktops in front of the windows. You will still need good artificial lighting for overcast days and at night.

A rise-and-fall lamp *right* can be raised for general illumination, or lowered to create an intimate glow. A crown-silvered bulb produces a tightly-focussed light beam, and helps prevent glare by masking the filament. Daylight levels can also be adjusted, thanks to the venetian blind.

Your first priority when it comes to kitchen lighting should be to ensure that you have safe and effective task lights close to all the main work areas in the room.

Task lighting is useful for directing light so that it falls in front of, rather than behind you, to prevent your shadow from obscuring the job at hand. The best way to install task lighting is to fit strip lights to the undersides of the wall cupboards or shelves above the worktop. Near the front of the units is ideal, but if this is not possible, place the lights towards the back; either way, they should be fitted with a baffle to cut down glare.

If there are no wall cupboards or shelves, above an island unit say, fix ceiling-mounted downlighters directly over the unit. General overhead lighting which is directed towards the floor need not be as bright or as even as task lighting, but it should allow you to see where you are going.

Light which bounces off the floor helps to illuminate the insides of open base cupboards – a good reason for choosing a pale floor in a dark room. Provide overhead lighting with recessed low-voltage fittings or spotlight tracks fixed to the ceiling. If you want to make a feature of the ceiling, use wall-mounted uplighters instead.

As in any other room, lighting can be used to add decorative character. A row of pendant fittings hung over a counter is just as effective as a bank of spotlights on the ceiling. Lights above a table can be controlled with a dimmer switch to allow you to change the mood when work stops and an evening meal begins. The dining table is the place to indulge your taste for the eccentric or theatrical. A chandelier suspended above the table brings a touch of glamour to an otherwise functional room, and candles at mealtimes create an aura of calm.

KITCHEN SAFETY

- Site ovens, stoves and grills away from windows; draughts can blow out gas flames or push curtains too near the heat source.

- Keep a fire extinguisher or fire blanket within easy reach of the stove at all times.

- If there are young children around, fit a high-level oven or choose a model with a door that is cool to the touch. Fit a metal guard around the stove to prevent toddlers from reaching hot pans.

- Fit child-resistant catches or locks to drawers and cupboards which contain sharp implements, chemicals, breakables and electrical items. Fit plastic corner protectors on sharp edges.

- Choose a non-slip floor and mop up spills straight away.

- Use anti-slip underlay beneath any loose rugs.

- When fixing shelves to plasterboard walls, ensure that screws are driven into the timber uprights inside. Freestanding shelves should be anchored firmly to the walls with a safety bracket.

LIGHT WORKS

Worktops are usually lit from sources concealed under wall-mounted cupboards. Create subtle lighting effects in other parts of the kitchen to stop your eyes getting tired.

CREATIVE STORAGE AND SHELVING

Cooking and eating are activities that seem to generate large amounts of rarely-used paraphernalia in a kitchen: special-occasion china; the 15-piece set of food processor blades; unwanted housewarming gifts; space for all this, and more, may have to be found somewhere.

Your first step should be to decide what you can live without. Editing the contents of your kitchen costs nothing, and it may be all you need to create more space. If you cannot bear to part with something, but haven't any use for it either, pack it securely in a clearly labelled box, then banish it to the basement or garage. Only constantly used items deserve a prime position in the kitchen, stored in a space somewhere between eye and knee level. Items which are used less frequently should be stored above or below this height. Remember to to take a regular look at your food cupboards too and throw away any stale foodstuffs.

Next, consider your existing or planned furniture layout. It may be that there is a narrow gap between two cupboards that can be fitted out with shelves or a bottle rack. The space between the base units and wall cabinets is easily put to good use; most kitchen manufacturers sell accessory-storage systems made up of rails and hooks, or magnetic strips, that enable you to keep knives and other essentials away from the worktop but close at hand.

Kitchen manufacturers are also a good source of ideas for making the most of cupboard and drawer interiors. Among the most useful are pull-out waste bins with two or more compartments for recycling, cutlery trays and attachments that allow easy storage of items such as plastic bags and vacuum cleaner hoses. Large base cupboards, such as the sink unit, benefit from being fitted out with extra pull-out trays and baskets for easier access to their contents. The idea can be adapted for the storage of linens, or fruit and vegetables. But it is especially useful when storing chemicals, to keep the risk of spillages to a minimum.

ON THE RAILS
left

Keep utensils and regularly-used condiments handy with an accessory rail fitted to the wall near the food preparation area and stove.

GLAZED SCREEN *below left*

A glazed cupboard provides storage for tableware close to where it is needed. Its size also gives the dining area a sense of enclosure.

DARK BACKGROUND
right

The side of a tall cupboard can be put to good use. Here, it has been built out to provide narrow shelving and hanging storage for cooking utensils and flavourings. The black surface contrasts well with the natural wood, and shows stainless steel utensils in a newly glamorous light.

STORAGE IDEAS

- Run a narrow shelf below a wall cupboard to store jars and other small containers.

- Instead of dotting appliances all over the worktop, group them on a sturdy triangular shelf in the corner. This should be fixed at a height that makes it possible to use both the shelf and the space beneath it.

- It may be possible to use the space behind the base plinth for drawers or to store shallow baking dishes or freezer containers.

- Ceiling-mounted racks and shelves can be used to store pans and cookery ingredients, as long as they're not too heavy. When there is a worktop underneath, they should be set at least 90cm (36in) above this, away from the edge of the worktop.

- If there is space between the end of a run of cabinets and the door, a corner shelf unit or wall-mounted hooks will allow you to use it for displaying good-looking equipment or decorative features such as flowers.

THE HUB OF THE HOME

The kitchen may be the traditional source of warmth and food, but it is also the place where a wide range of other, equally pleasurable, activities takes place. It might be where you host the weekly card game with friends, oversee children's hobbies, or plant seeds for next summer's borders. Space for more routine tasks, such as recycling, laundry and paying the bills, may be needed too. And underscoring it all may be the familiar drone of the radio, hi-fi or television. Young children in particular love being where their parents are, and they often become permanent features of a family kitchen, together with their toys. When they are babies, space needs to be found for a highchair and small toys. The former could slot under the dining table when not in use, along with a box on wheels that keeps wipes, clean bibs and toys close at hand. As they get older, the table will be commandeered for artistic activities, and a wipe-clean tablecloth with pockets at each corner for crayons and colouring books may come in handy. Art materials can also be stored on a low shelf or drawer, to make it easier for the children to retrieve them — and put them away.

Preparing and cooking food generates large amounts of waste, so the kitchen is a good place for housing a recycling area. If, however, you have spare space in a garage or outside the back door perhaps, by all means site it there. The main purpose of a recycling area is to make it easy for you to sort rubbish according to type: organic waste for composting, newspaper, white paper, aluminium cans, tin cans, light bulbs, string, batteries, plastics such as PET, and the three most common glass colours, green, brown and clear, need to be separated before they can be collected or disposed of.

Breakables should be put into rigid containers, such as cardboard boxes or polypropylene bins. And heavier categories of waste, such as glass and newspaper, are best sited on or near the floor, so that bundles or boxes can be slid easily onto a utility cart. The rest can be stored on shelves, where they take up surprisingly little

space; you need an awful lot of light bulbs to fill a shoebox, while many plastic bottles and aluminium cans can be crushed to a fraction of their former volume. Dangerous waste, such as chemicals, should obviously be stored in a secure box, out of children's reach.

An American survey recently uncovered the fact that eighty per cent of kitchens double as home workspaces. If you need a separate desk for business or homework, try to site it away from the food preparation area. Consider also its position in relation to the door and window. Natural light is nicer to work by, but a view of the outdoors may distract rather than inspire.

Even if you are happy doing household accounts on the kitchen table, some form of storage for domestic paperwork is always useful. This can take the form of a drawer dedicated to the purpose, or a concertina file that allows you to organize the contents by subject or by month.

With so much to think about, it's easy to forget that kitchens are for relaxing too. You may prefer to find room for a comfortable armchair and a reading light, or a cutting block so that two people can work and talk at the same time. Home entertainment equipment, such as the hi-fi and television, should be sited away from the stove and sink, ideally on an eye-level shelf so that they won't get covered with food.

ENTERTAINING IN THE KITCHEN

Space for an impromptu supper for eight can be found in all but the smallest kitchens, as long as you bear in mind the possibility when you are choosing the furniture. Firstly, look for a table with extension leaves, or a gateleg design with fold-down flaps, as these can easily be expanded to accommodate anything from four to ten people. Look out also for chairs which fold or stack easily; those that are not in daily use can be stored in another part of the house, or hung on wall-mounted pegs if they are light enough.

Alternatively, you may be able to bring in extra chairs from elsewhere. A rattan armchair, such as the one shown here, is compact enough to slide under a dining table when not being used in a living room or bedroom. You may have to pad it out with an extra cushion.

Even the most casual get-together becomes a party when the table is dressed for the occasion. Homework and newspapers should be cleared away and replaced by a tablecloth or place mats, napkins, and a simple centrepiece, such as a bowl of fruit or a vase of fresh flowers.

EATING IN THE KITCHEN

The advantages of eating in the kitchen are obvious. The business of preparing and cooking food becomes a shared experience, rather than one person's drudgery; food can be moved from the stove to the table with the minimum of effort. And removing the need for a separate dining room means that you can create more space elsewhere.

Take your time when choosing kitchen furniture. It should be comfortable, since you can often spend several hours sitting in the same

Alternatively, seating around part of the table can be provided by benches or banquettes. While these are less easy to move around, they can accommodate a varying number of people, and they often provide generous extra storage space under the seats.

Simple styles of furniture suit kitchens best; they can always be dressed up with linen and accessories for special occasions. If you want to give a dining area greater presence, try and find space for a dresser or buffet nearby. As well as

WINDOW SEATS

When the table is placed adjacent to a working area, the chairs should tuck neatly underneath it when they're not in use *left*.

A chequerboard floor is teamed with red walls to create a strong yet welcoming look *right*. Pendant light fittings hung low over the table add brightness to what might otherwise be a gloomy room.

chair over the course of a day. Tables especially, should be robust enough to withstand regular abuse; surfaces need to wipe clean, and chairs need to be strong enough to lean back in or stand on. There should be sufficient elbow room for everyone around the table, and space to move around its edges if it is pushed into a corner to enlarge the room.

making the room look more furnished, it can be used for decorative displays.

Kitchens also need to cope with a constant flow of people wanting a snack, and this is where a breakfast bar or folding table is useful. If it can be sited out of the cook's way, but with easy access to the refrigerator and microwave, then so much the better.

USING FABRIC AND FINISHING TOUCHES

- Fabrics help to soften the mood in a room which is often filled with hard and shiny surfaces. They can also be used to enliven a bland scheme, or add freshness to a room that feels too dark or too warm.

- Use fabric in the form of accessories: chairs can be dressed up with tie-on squab cushions or slipcovers; runners, napkins, tea cosies, and fabric-lined bread baskets are all practical finishing touches for a dresser or table.

- A rug or mat helps to anchor and define a sitting area in an open-plan kitchen. Designs which incorporate a small motif or a tweedy texture can help to disguise food and drink stains. Flat-weave and short, densely-woven carpet textures are the easiest types to brush down.

- Kitchen windows benefit most from unfussy and practical treatments. Consider wipe-clean roller blinds, or easily removable café curtains. Suitable fabrics include: light cottons, calico, canvas, linen (plain tea towels sewn together look especially smart) and net.

- Store textiles in a scented drawer to keep them free from food smells. A shelf or window-sill by the table is useful for storing everyday napkins and condiments.

WINDOW VIEW
A small folding table set next to a window can be used temporarily for work or reading, as well as for intimate meals.

KITCHEN LIVING

Being able to socialize with family or friends while you cook sounds wonderful in theory, but you may not want guests to know that their supper came out of a packet. And companions are unlikely to feel relaxed if their view is of counters covered in washing-up and cooking debris. There is no doubt that cooking, eating and relaxation become even more enjoyable when they can be combined, but there is nothing life-enhancing about a kitchen that does not allow you to do any of these things properly.

The secret of successful living in the kitchen is, inevitably, having enough space for everyone to fit in and be able to spread out. The amount of space needed depends on what the room is to be used for; a small area for family meals is a lot easier to accommodate than an all-purpose living space, complete with armchairs, a sofa and a television.

The ideal arrangement is one where the cooking and eating or relaxing areas are visually linked, yet clearly distinguishable from one another. It may be that the shape of the room suggests a natural dividing line; a bay window or alcove, for example, is a good place to site the table or a sofa because it gives it a sense of enclosure, and allows you to keep the business part of the room clear. If you have knocked through into an adjacent room to make the kitchen larger, then the remains of the old dividing wall, such as beams or an archway, can be used to define each area.

THE SIMPLE APPROACH *above left*

Little touches make all the difference. Siting the table near a window gives it a different mood, and so helps to separate it from the rest of the kitchen.

Blackboard paint makes a stylish yet practical wallcovering *below left*, especially when there are young children about. Even adults would not resist the temptation to scribble once in a while.

A metal table and spun-aluminium lampshades visually link the dining area with the rest of a modern kitchen *right*.

CARING FOR KITCHEN SURFACES

- Use liquid detergent or a non-scratch cleaner to clean laminated surfaces. It is difficult to remove scratches without damaging the surface further.

- Solid wood and veneered surfaces should be wiped down regularly with a slightly damp cloth. Once every six months, seal with a linseed-oil based compound to protect them from damp and stains. Burn marks and scratches can be removed or reduced with sandpaper.

- Painted walls and cupboards can be washed with a mild detergent solution on a soft cloth.

- Stainless steel is best cleaned with bicarbonate of soda. Prolonged contact with cleaners that contain bleach, and carbon steel objects, causes corrosion.

- Glazed ceramic tiles and mosaics can be cleaned with a damp cloth. Terracotta and quarry tiles should be waxed or oiled after installation, and then at yearly intervals, to protect them from food stains.

- Marble pastry boards should be scrubbed with a non-acid cleaner. Darker coloured marble will hide the inevitable stains better.

CHAPTER THREE

BEDROOMS

Bedrooms are all about rest, relaxation and successful storage. A sensitive approach to decoration, with few soft furnishings, muted colours and clutter-free surfaces will ensure a healthy environment for deep sleep.

Create romance with careful lighting, invitingly crisp bedlinen and finishing touches such as flowers and natural scents. Banish dust by stripping floorboards, adding rugs and leaving space beneath the bed for it to breathe.

Look here for ideas on ingenious storage solutions, window treatments and tips for dressing a bed, as well as one-room living and flexible furniture.

THE ROMANTIC BEDROOM

Romance is a state of mind rather than a decorating style, and there is no law which says a room can look romantic only if its furnishings are feminine and frilly. It is true that the idea of a romantic bedroom does appeal to women more than men, but there are ways of making rooms feel sensual and fun without them looking too fussy. In decoration, as in life, it is all about doing what feels right, and allowing yourself to revel in the pleasure of making sympathetic objects and surfaces work together.

Nostalgia plays a big part in the creation of a romantic bedroom. The country cottage is a favourite, with its chalky pastels, homely linens and touches of lace, as is Gothic decoration,

often expressed as richly patterned surfaces, gilt or brass accessories and turned wood. Look for handcrafted surfaces and objects, such as embroidered bedlinen and handmade rugs.

In romantic bedrooms, layered colours and textures are a key part of the look. Combine pillows and duvets with bedspreads and throw pillows. Side-tables might hold books, treasured objects or family photographs and flowers. At the window, simple curtains can be dressed up with a patterned voile fabric underneath and contrasting tie-backs. There is always a danger of this look becoming cluttered, so use a narrow colour range and group objects into collections to maintain some coherence.

SOFT AND GENTLE *above*

Classic Swedish country style is effortlessly romantic in a room with warm wooden panelling and a sheer lace bed canopy.

DRESSED FOR BED *right*

A welcoming and romantic bedroom does not have to be all white lace and muslin. Here a boldly-coloured wall and a simple blind make the perfect backdrop for multi-layered and richly-textured bedlinen on a tall bed.

THE SIMPLE BEDROOM

A simply decorated bedroom is where we seek relief from the stresses of daily life. Like all retreats, it should be designed to calm the senses and clear the mind; there are no unnecessary distractions here. Colour, pattern and furnishings are kept to a minimum, and surfaces are chosen for their inherent beauty, not hidden under massed ranks of pictures and clutter. The room should not look like a barren and soulless monk's cell though; creating the right atmosphere and a sense of comfort still matters.

Much of the decorative interest should be created by contrasts of texture and form, since colour and pattern will play a fairly limited role here. You might, for example, use a curvy headboard in a boxy room, or dress a rustic bed with beautifully embroidered white linen. Simply-themed rooms do not always have to be decorated in shades of white or neutrals; using small amounts of dark or strong colour as an accent prevents a scheme from looking overly dull and washed-out.

CALM SPIRIT

Dramatic architecture rarely calls for a fussy or complex decorative approach. The furniture in this bedroom under the roof, *above*, has been chosen wisely for its ability to look unobtrusive yet welcoming. Minimal curtains allow the distinctive windows to speak for themselves.

Simple furnishings are ideal for smaller rooms, as they can help create an impression of space, *right*. To maintain the pared-down feel, space for storage is found wherever possible; in bedside tables, a blanket chest, the window-seat and under the bed.

THE HEALTHY BEDROOM

Planning a bedroom so that it contributes to your overall well-being is important. Most of us prefer to sleep at the back of the house, away from street lights and noise, and we instinctively position the bed where it affords us the best view of anyone entering the room. In addition, sleeping in a room that catches the early morning sun allows you to wake more naturally.

The most healthy mattress fillings are those made from natural fibres such as cotton and wool. Avoid mattresses made from polyurethane foam; if they catch fire they release highly toxic fumes. Many mattresses are treated with a flame retardant which contains formaldehyde, a potent irritant and allergen. You can reduce the amount of fumes they release by covering the mattress with a wool underblanket or natural fleece.

Metal-sprung bed bases and bedsteads acquire a weak electric charge over time, and start to emit electro-magnetic fields (EMFs) which may lead to disturbed sleep at night and listlessness by day. It is possible to minimize the effects of EMFs by placing a special neutralizing undersheet directly over the mattress.

Paint can be a lingering source of toxic fumes, and not just when it's freshly applied. In particular, try to limit the amount of oil-based gloss paint used in the bedroom; instead, use water-based emulsion for the walls, and natural varnishes, waxes or stains for woodwork and floorboards. Beware also of 'non-iron' or 'crease-free' bedlinen, as these have often been treated with formaldehyde. Try to keep window treatments simple and decorative clutter to a minimum, as both attract dust, another common allergen.

A bedroom may be unhealthy simply because it is too warm – an air temperature of between 55 and 60°F is ideal for most adults. However, it should be two or three degrees warmer in rooms which are occupied by the very young or the elderly, or if you suffer from respiratory difficulties such as asthma.

NATURAL COLOUR *right*

Sleeping between sheets made from natural fabrics isn't just healthy, it feels nicer too. Look out also for linens and blankets coloured with vegetable dyes – shades of yellow, orange, brown and grey predominate, but purples and blues are also available. When painting furniture, use products made from plants, minerals and resin oils.

THE LOW-ALLERGY BEDROOM

- If possible, buy bedclothes made from untreated natural fabrics. Wash all new bedding in non-biological laundry detergent before you use it.

- If you are sensitive to duvets filled with natural down or feathers, try cotton kapok instead or use 100 per cent cotton sheets and blankets.

- If you are allergic to a wool-filled mattress, use one made from latex foam instead.

- Keep dust and house mites under control by resting the bed mattress on a slatted wood base, and keeping the area under the bed clear. This makes it easier for moisture to escape from the mattress and bedlinen.

- Alternatively, use a futon bed, but always roll or fold the mattress when not in use, so as to expose more of the surface to the air.

- Always turn back duvets and other bed coverings during the day.

- Use organic products to seal and stain wooden floorboards. If you want a wall-to-wall carpet, choose one which is made from 100 per cent wool. Even these are sometimes treated with mothproofing and soil repellants, so if you are sensitive to them, steam-clean the carpet with plain water immediately after installation.

- Wherever possible, furniture should be made from natural materials and finished with non-toxic paints or polishes.

CLEAN AND HEALTHY

It's not always necessary to add colour to a room, especially when attractive contrasts are created by natural materials.

PLANNING THE SPACE

Bedrooms are rarely used only for sleeping. They may also have to double up as a study, a second living room or as an exercise area. It is a lot to ask of somewhere which is sometimes barely big enough to accommodate a bed, so careful planning is essential.

The bed is likely to be the largest item of furniture here, and in an average-sized room it needs to be placed where it allows maximum movement around the space.

Pushing it into a corner may well give you more floor space, but this has to be balanced against the problems that it invariably creates,

such as making it awkward for two people to use the bed, and allowing space for only one bedside table. However, it can work extremely well for single beds, especially if they are built into a wall of cupboards to create an enclosed box-bed effect.

Matters are often complicated by the fact that we need to store large amounts of clothing, shoes and household linens in the bedroom. Chests of drawers, blanket chests and dressing tables can help, but a run of built-in cupboards is often the only practical answer. Unfortunately, it is not always the most attractive solu-

tion, as large-scale built-in furniture can easily dominate a small room.

The answer may be to create a dressing area divided off from the rest of the room by screens or a partition. This is not as difficult as it sounds: a non-structural wall can be made easily from timber battens and plasterboard, both of which are available from DIY stores. The fake wall can be slotted into a remarkably small area (see plan). Concealed but open storage such as this reduces the need for space-hungry doors. A less permanent alternative would be to use a folding screen made from particleboard panels.

PLAN OF BEDROOM

A partition screens clothes storage and the dressing area from view. The space between the cupboards and the wall can be as little as 60cm (24in) wide.

Lamps fixed to the wall allow smaller bedside tables to be used.

Fix a mirror to the top of a chest of drawers to transform it into a dressing table.

A lounger is useful for providing versatile, additional seating.

A wood-floor and cotton rugs help to reduce the build-up of dust.

PANELLED ATTIC *above*

Delicate furniture, light textiles and an all-over panelled treatment for the walls and ceiling help to create a feeling of spaciousness in an attic bedroom.

PLANNING SMALL OR AWKWARDLY-SHAPED BEDROOMS

Finding ways to make a bed appear less obvious is the key to planning small or awkwardly-shaped bedrooms. Sofa beds and futons, which roll up or fold away, are worth considering as they allow you to use the bed space for other activities during the day. The disadvantages are that area needs to be found for bedding during the day, and the physical act of making and unmaking your bed twice a day, every day, very soon becomes a chore.

Alternatively, it may be possible to raise the height of the bed, by siting it on a sleeping platform. This keeps the sleeping area hidden from view, and increases the amount of usable floor space in the room. A sleeping platform calls for a minimum ceiling height of around 2.5m (8ft) to be feasible, although a height of 2.7m (8½ft) or more is desirable.

BUILT-IN FURNITURE

- When buying wardrobes, bear in mind that coats and dresses should hang in a space which is 1.5m (5ft) high, while shirts and separates need 1m (3ft 4in). If you have space for only one hanging rail, make it 1.7m (6ft) high, and use the area underneath the clothes for storing shoe racks, shelves, a drawer trolley or stacking boxes.

- Ideally, the space between the front of a wardrobe and other furniture should measure at least 60cm (24in). This gap can be reduced slightly if the wardrobe is fitted with folding or sliding doors.

- Allow yourself plenty of drawer and shelf space for storing sweaters, t-shirts, socks and underwear, as well as spare bedding and linen. As a rule, there should be slightly more space given over to drawers and shelves than to hanging rails.

- Make the most of built-in wardrobes by hanging ties and belts on hooks fixed to the insides of doors.

- Shallow areas such as alcoves can usually be turned into wardrobes by fitting cupboards which are 35cm (14in) deep.

- Fit cupboards from floor to ceiling wherever possible. Use the uppermost shelves for storing rarely-used and non-seasonal items. Store seldom-used garments in sealed bags or lidded boxes to protect them from dust.

AWKWARD CORNER

Drawers slotted under a window-seat and the bed demonstrate how built-in storage makes the most of small areas.

ATTENTION TO DETAIL

SQUARE DANCE

When mixing two or more patterns, it helps if the same colours appear in each one *above*. The cheerful bed-linen suggested a possible colour scheme for the room *right*.

A transparent curtain offers privacy without cutting out too much light *far right*. The tie-back was made by sewing strips of fabric together until it measured three times the distance from the curtain pole to the floor. The fabric was folded lengthways, sewn along the longest edge, and turned inside out.

If you find it hard to select a wall colour for your bedroom, why not use a pattern as your starting point instead? Even the humble check can be a rich source of inspiration. Here, it appears in many forms and sizes: the small criss-cross effect created by the woven headboard is repeated in the lounger, but is also subtly echoed in the square wooden panelling on the lower part of the walls. Meanwhile, the cheerful bed-linen fabric suggested the colour scheme for both the walls and the curtain.

Decorating with pattern is often thought to be risky and difficult, but it need not be if you keep to linear or geometric patterns such as classic checks and stripes, or simple all-over motifs such as stars and polka dots. If you've never used pattern before, start off by adding it, in small amounts, into a room decorated in plain colours. Introduce the pattern in the form of accessories and soft furnishings to bring a dull corner to life.

As your confidence grows, try mixing different sizes and styles of the same pattern, as here. The secret is to use only a narrow range of colours, so that the end result looks lively without being overpowering.

Like colour, pattern can be used either as an accent or as the major element of a decorative scheme. It is most often used to break up large areas, such as a bed or a floor. The size or scale of the pattern you use is critical; large patterns, like bright colours, draw the eye inwards, so they can make a large room seem cosier. They are stimulating rather than relaxing, so may not be suitable for a bedroom. Small-scale patterns appear to recede and are useful for making small rooms seem larger, but they can be bland and insignificant unless they form part of an unusual colour scheme.

STORAGE

It doesn't matter where you store your clothes as long as you organize the space well; you can use a freestanding wardrobe or open rails, sleekly fitted cupboards or an ad hoc collection of junk shop finds. What counts is whether the storage is flexible enough to adapt to the ebb and flow of accummulated possessions.

First take a critical look at what needs to be stored. Group similar items, such as sweaters or jackets, together. Next, divide each category into three: items which are in current use, non-seasonal items, and those which haven't seen the light of day for a year or more. The first group should be the only one to make it onto your shelves and rails. The second group can be stored in sealed bags at the top of the wardrobe until the weather changes. And unless you have a very good reason, the last group of belongings should be discarded.

Most categories of clothing can be stored in a variety of ways. Sweaters, jeans and t-shirts, for example, can be kept in baskets, drawers or shelves. The methods you choose will depend on your budget and the space available, but check that shelves and rails can be moved easily.

TIDY ENDINGS

left Modular storage systems are ideal when you need to store a wide variety of objects in one place. To make access easier, regularly-worn clothes and shoes should be stored within easy reach, while spare bedding, towels and less frequently-used items are kept on higher shelves. A wheeled unit is useful for dirty laundry.
right A neater finish is achieved by using wardrobes with interior fittings. Once the hanging rails are set at the right height, the space around them can be allocated to shelves and drawers. Large shelves should be kept tidy by housing items in baskets or boxes, while the doors and walls are fitted with hooks or pegs for accessories, such as belts, ties and scarves.

CARING FOR CLOTHES

- Hang tailored garments on contoured wooden or plastic hangers. Wire hangers bend easily out of shape and are more likely to snag clothes. Padded hangers help keep delicate fabrics, such as lace or silk, in good shape.

- Keep shirts, blouses, skirts and jackets buttoned up to reduce wrinkling. Trousers should be left unbuttoned, but folded along the front and back creases.

- Avoid storing clothes in plastic bags for long periods, as the chemicals in the plastic can leach into fabrics. To guard against moths, wrap clothes in tissue paper.

- Small garments, such as stockings, are best stored in small boxes or baskets, or in divided drawers, to stop them from becoming tangled and unruly. Organize jewellery by placing it in boxes or drawers divided into small fabric-lined compartments.

- With the exception of sneakers (sports shoes) and sandals, all shoes should be stored on a wooden tree or packed with tissue paper inside. Try not to wear the same pair of shoes every day, as this prevents them from drying out and regaining their shape.

- Keep sewing and shoe-care kits handy and well-stocked.

A PLACE FOR EVERYTHING

Equip a walk-in wardrobe with a mixture of wooden shelves on brackets and open canvas shelves which hang from a rail.

FLEXIBLE FURNITURE

As beds often take up large chunks of floor area, the remaining furniture in the bedroom needs to be easy to use in confined spaces. The area immediately around the bed is often only just wide enough to move around in, and if there is any space left over, it may well have to be shared between several activities such as dressing, relaxing and study or exercise. This can be made much easier if the furniture is compact, light and flexible. It also helps if it looks light, to contrast with the block-like bed.

The obvious advantage of compact furniture is its ability to fit into small and awkward corners. A bedside table needs to be only 30cm (12in) or so across and 40cm (16in) deep to provide enough space for a clock, a glass of water and some reading matter. If storage space is in short supply, it may make more sense to use small office filing cabinets or bookshelves instead of conventional tables. The seat of a stool or chair also makes a good bedside surface, as long as it is reasonably flat. If it stacks or folds for storage, so much the better.

Furniture that can be moved easily from one place to another also helps to make better use of the space. In a studio bedroom, a low table or box on wheels can be used as a coffee table during the day, but be pushed to one side when it is time for bed. If you want to use part of the room for another activity, say a dressing area or a workspace, a panelled screen will create an instant sense of intimacy and enclosure. It will also help hide the inevitable clutter.

A screen will also lend a little of its elegance to a small or boxy room. Its undulating form adds architectural interest to an uninspiring space. If it is high enough, it can be placed in front of a window instead of curtains. If you don't plan to stay in one home for very long, a screen can save you having to spend money on blinds or curtains.

For defining the boundaries of a work or dressing area on a more permanent basis, use freestanding shelving or bookcases, as they will provide storage as well as screening. Try to use

furniture that looks good from all sides, and not just the front. Open shelves or pigeonholes work best, as they offer tantalizing glimpses of the area on the other side of the screen. If you use a unit with a back, try and blend the back of it with the rest of your scheme, by painting it the same colour as the walls, perhaps, or using it to display pictures.

Storage can also be portable: trolleys and butler's tray tables are invaluable when it comes to organizing lots of small items such as toiletries or office stationery. Pigeonhole units on wheels make a good alternative to shelves if you are refitting out the interior of an old built-in wardrobe. And if you have no space for a

blanket chest, try storing bedding in sturdy baskets or crates. Laundry bags and valet stands can often be folded away when not in use, and if you have high-level cupboards or shelves, it may be worth investing in a set of folding steps.

Multi-purpose furniture is always versatile. Lightweight armchairs made of rattan or wicker can easily be pressed into service if extra seating is required in the living or dining room. If you have space, a daybed or *chaise longue* can be used for both sitting and reclining on. Trunks and blanket chests double up as storage areas and low tables; if a squab cushion can be fixed temporarily to the top of them, they will also provide occasional seating.

MULTI-PURPOSE BEDROOMS

A ROOM FOR EVERYTHING

A work or dressing area by a window can be screened off when not in use *left*.

Turning the room into a daytime retreat *below left* can be as simple as finding a space for a comfortable chair. Siting it near a window allows you to read by daylight.

A mobile home-entertainment centre *below* can be wheeled to where it is needed or else tucked away in a corner.

The bedroom *right* also houses exercise equipment.

CREATING LEISURE SPACE

- Folding tables and chairs allow you to create a temporary desk in the bedroom. Make yourself comfortable: look for a chair design that allows you to sit upright; you can adjust the height of the seat with a tie-on squab cushion. Also, ensure that the tabletop is smooth and stable if it is to be used for working on.

- Keep stationery to hand in attractive boxes or lidded baskets.

- To make exercise less of a chore, dedicate a space in a wardrobe or chest of drawers to the storage of paraphernalia such as hand weights, water bottles and workout videos. Alternatively, find an old gym locker and place it by the equipment or machines.

- Sports equipment such as rackets and bats can be hung on metal racks made for the purpose, and hooks fixed inside a cupboard door, or stored in an umbrella stand or deep wastepaper basket.

- Fix a mirror and pegs for towels on a wall so they are near your exercise equipment.

DRESSING THE BED

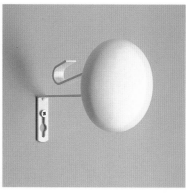

1 FITTING DRAPE HOOKS

Mark the position of the drape hooks on the wall with a pencil and fix them in position, using a screwdriver.

2 DRAPING THE FABRIC

Place a large corner of the fabric over one of the end drape hooks and temporarily fix in place. Ask someone to hold it for you or, alternatively, pin it in position temporarily.

3 ATTACHING RIBBON

Cut 3 lengths of ribbon, each 2m (2yds) long and tie the first one tightly around an end drape hook, securing the fabric firmly in place.

A flat panel of fabric can be turned into an impressive bed hanging within minutes. For a really quick and simple solution, use a patterned or plain double sheet. Here we used 4m (4yds) of striped fabric, cut into half to form two pieces, each 2m (2yds) long x 1.5m (5ft) wide. They were sewn together by machine-hemming the raw edges on the wrong side of the fabric. Bows in a contrasting striped fabric provide a neat finishing touch.

MATERIALS

4m (4yds) fabric

3 drape hooks

Pencil

3 rawlplugs, 3 screws

Screwdriver

Sewing thread

Pins (optional)

2m (2yds) ribbon

4 TIE-ING THE BOWS

Drape the fabric in a generous fold between the first hook and the next. Repeat for the other hooks. When all 3 hooks are covered with fabric, and secured with ribbon, tie a bow on each one.

USING FABRIC

A simple bed hanging is quick and easy to make *opposite*. Eco-friendly bedlinen contrasts well with a galvanized steel drawer cabinet used as a bedside table *left*. Lengths of fabric hung from a coronet-style rail create a feminine feel *top*. Fabric headboards don't have to be fussy: here, a button-on design is tailored yet comfortable look *above*.

FINISHING TOUCHES

EASY LUXURY *left*

A narrow table on wheels is the perfect perch for books and a breakfast tray on lazy days. At other times, it can be placed at the end of the bed or against a wall, and put to a variety of uses, as a display area for blankets, or as a dressing table.

SIMPLE COMFORTS *right*

Carefully added colour helps to ensure that this minimally-furnished room looks welcoming rather than spartan. Cushions and a simple tablecloth soften the lines of the skeletal furniture, and their colours act as a bridge between the bold rug and the picture.

The more simple your bedroom scheme, the more important it is to get the details right. If you plan to hang only one picture on the wall, make sure it can bear such strong emphasis. Similarly, if the reading lamp is the only object on your bedside table, it needs to have some decorative merit of its own in addition to providing a good light source. Adding finishing touches to a room should not mean filling it with distracting clutter; it is more about selecting and displaying those objects which say something about your personal style.

If you have the space, a small table or chest of drawers can be an extremely useful piece of furniture. It not only gives you a surface on which to display a decorative object or two, but also acts as a convenient resting point for a news-

paper or the breakfast tray. If a mirror is hung on the wall above it, or placed directly on the surface, it can be used as a dressing table. To make life easier, use a mirror that tilts or swivels to suit the height of the person using it, and add lights which illuminate the face evenly from the front, not from above or below.

The bedroom, as a personal space, is a favourite location for displaying framed photographs of friends and loved ones. Grouping them on the wall or on a surface of some kind gives them added impact. Place them out of direct sunlight, as it will fade the colours.

If you like to display lots of pictures, but don't want to riddle your freshly painted walls with holes, try placing your images on narrow shelves. These can easily be made by screwing

75mm- (3in-) deep shelves directly into the wall, or better still, onto shelf supports. The top surface should be grooved, or fitted with a lip at the front to stop pictures sliding forward.

Although it doesn't sound like half as much fun, remember also to pay attention to fittings, such as door handles and light switches. A door knob that turns easily and fits your hand snugly, and hinges that operate soundlessly, come under the category of things that make life easier. Tired-looking cupboards and chests of drawers can be given a totally new look simply by changing the knobs or pulls. They need not match; try mixing black and white knobs on a set of drawers for a harlequin effect. Power sockets and wastepaper baskets, on the other hand, should be as discreet as possible.

WINDOW TREATMENTS

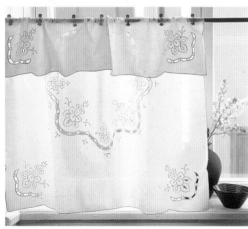

FRAMING THE VIEW

top In a romantically-furnished room, sill-length drapes are given a touch of style with a looped heading threaded on to a brass pole. The blue and white check fabric has a homely feel, like the simple, traditional furniture placed nearby.

above Antique napkins can be turned into pretty curtains by fixing them to a narrow café curtain rod with curtain clips.

opposite To create the easiest ever window treatment, throw a length of fabric over a pole and tie a large knot in the front section to allow light to filter through from behind. The length of the fabric should measure slightly more than twice the distance between the pole and the floor.

left When maximizing daylight levels is not a priority, fabrics can be layered at a window. Rather than exclude the light completely, this effect infuses the area around the window with a soft glow.

above Window treatments which are tailored to fit unusually-shaped windows can be prohibitively expensive. Here, the solution is to screen only the rectangular portion of the window, with a fabric panel slung over net curtain wire.

ONE-ROOM LIVING

STORAGE SOLUTIONS

left A wall of cupboards keeps clutter under wraps in an open-plan space, while low metal shelving provides display space. The latter's open structure makes it easier to see through, and so avoids a hemmed-in feeling. It may not be in the ideal position here, but there's no real reason why a favourite object, such as a bicycle, should not be displayed boldly.

LAYERED LAYOUT

right A sleeping platform allows the bed to be tucked away out of sight and leaves precious floor space free for work and other activities. Even narrow spaces, such as a lobby or the wall between two windows, can be fitted with shelves or cupboards. Compact furniture is easy to move when it is time to unfold the sofabed.

Fitting a wide range of activities into one room, no matter how large or small it is, requires you to make imaginative and efficient use of the space. The furniture you choose may well have to be multi-purpose, and storage needs to be squeezed in wherever there happens to be any spare space.

As always, your first task is to organize the space. The room's shape will help you do this, especially if there are changes in level, perhaps in the form of a raised area near a window, and fixed points of interest, such as a fireplace. The position of the kitchen may well be determined by the location of the existing power and water supplies, or the need for an extractor fan.

Changes in level are a good idea, because they allow you to use the full height of the space, and help create several smaller areas within the same room. Placing the bed on a sleeping platform is one of the easiest and cheapest ways to do this. On the other hand, if the ceiling is high enough, it may be possible to create a galleried seating or storage area. The space underneath a raised floor can often be used for storage.

Using the furniture as screening also works well. Large pieces, such as a sofabed or book-shelves, can be used as room dividers. If space is very tight, similar results can be achieved with blinds fixed to the ceiling, or a folding screen.

In multi-purpose spaces, adequate storage is essential, as you often need to tidy away the evidence of one activity before you can enjoy another. If the shape of your room allows it, build a wall of floor-to-ceiling cupboards that hides everything, including the television and the kitchen sink. Awkward areas, such as the space under the stairs, can be kitted out with shelves, cupboards or drawers. Look out also for styles of furniture that incorporate storage.

In general, it is best to restrict your colour palette and use the same decorative approach throughout the room. You are less likely to tire of neutral backgrounds, but a splash of colour or pattern is often a welcome diversion.

TEENAGE BEDROOMS

SELF-CONTAINED *above*

A teenager's room needs to be a place where he or she can work, pursue interests, entertain friends and begin to explore his or her own sense of style – without fear of interference from other members of the family. When decorating a room for a teenage child, a parent's role should be to provide sturdy furniture, basic bedding and soft furnishings. Once this is done, they should withdraw gracefully.

SECRET DRAWERS *left*

Most teenagers prefer to make up their own minds about where and how to display favourite possessions, but modular storage units can help to organize work, hobbies and secret collections.

ROOM TO GROOVE *left*

Having friends to stay is a passion that endures well into adolescence. Bunk beds are worth considering in a small room, to leave more floor space for chilling out, listening to music and proudly displaying your latest acquisitions. Few adults, let alone teenagers, achieve this level of tidiness, but incorporating one or two items of built-in furniture will provide some incentive.

ON DISPLAY *above*

Most young people regard storage and display as one and the same. Heavy items, such as books or the television and hi-fi, are stored for safety's sake on sturdy shelving, while smaller objects are displayed in an under-used corner, another sound way of keeping them free from harm.

CHAPTER FOUR

BATHROOMS

Whether a tiny windowless room or a former bedroom with acres of space, a bathroom demands to be functional. Surfaces need to be water-resistant, safety and storage are priorities and, for comfort's sake, pay close attention to your heating, lighting and ventilation needs.

As it is usually one of the smallest and least lived-in rooms in the home, you can allow your decorative ambitions to go wild. Use strong colour on walls and towels, bold shelving ideas and specific themes. Indulge your whims and yourself in a space which should be fun, absorbing and inspiring.

THE WELL-ORDERED BATHROOM

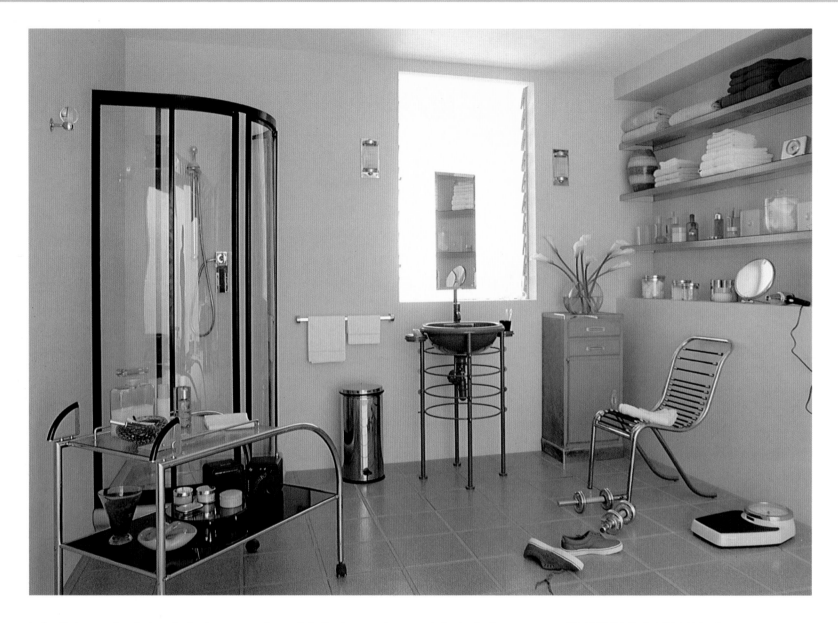

In family homes the design of a bathroom needs to reflect the fact that it is a shared space. Each member of the family should be able to use the bathroom safely and comfortably, and space needs to be found for storing toiletries, towels, bath accessories and toys.

Everything has to fit into what is often left-over space; a corner of an attic conversion, perhaps, or a windowless box created by dividing up a larger room. Creating storage thus becomes a matter of making creative use of the space around fittings and exploiting walls to the full. Putting panels around the bath, for example, creates shelf space, while sinks and toilets can be incorporated into modular or built-in cabinets. For a less fitted look, consider using open shelving, freestanding cabinets and trolleys. Make life easier for children and the elderly by fitting hand grips close to the bath.

To ease the rush at certain times of day, it may be worth screening off the shower or bath area, or adding an extra sink, so more than one person can use the room at the same time. A separate toilet helps to avoid traffic jams.

FLEXIBLE OPTIONS *above*

Open shelves provide a decorative display area for towels and toiletries, while a trolley provides extra storage space for bath accessories, which can be wheeled to wherever it is needed.

STREAMLINED SENSE *right*

Built-in cupboards make good use of tight spaces, and raising them off the floor helps to avoid a hemmed-in feeling. A hanging storage rail helps to keep the area around the bath and sink well organized and clutter-free.

THE ATMOSPHERIC BATHROOM

Bathrooms are not used solely for a hurried shower before you leave for work or school. They are also places where you can relax, have fun, groom or beautify, and have a chance to be self-indulgent. Fantasy or dramatic decorative themes can prove particularly successful in bathrooms as we do not spend a significant amount of time here each day. And as they are relatively small, they offer scope for using more unusual treatments, such as mosaic and murals, which can look over-the-top in larger rooms.

Some form of screening at the window may be necessary. The simplest way to do this is by fitting window-panes of etched or frosted glass. The latter is available in a wide variety of patterns, while the former can be customized to your own design — a striped pattern or a porthole of clear glass in an etched window looks spectacular, and can be ordered from a glass merchant. Stained glass windows fill rooms with ever-changing shadows and colours, but they are expensive, so are only worth considering for small areas.

For a softer effect, use fabric or wooden blinds, shutters, a café curtain on the lower part of a tall window, or softly gathered voile. Lights should be positioned so that you are not silhouetted against the window at night — try to arrange them around the edges of the room, not in the centre. If you are in no danger of being overlooked, you may not need screening at all. After all, what could be nicer than a bath with a view?

Most people are nervous about making a decorative statement in small spaces, but it is well worth doing. After all, if the alternative is bare walls that close in on you, why not create something that is really worth looking at? Strong colour contrasts and textured surfaces such as mosaic or sealed plaster, contrast well with smooth bathroom fittings. A touch of fantasy can be welcome too; walls can be painted with murals based on watery themes, or panelled to suggest log cabins and beach huts.

SPLASHDOWN *opposite*

A raised bath with steps leading up to it turns bathtime into an adventure. On a more practical note, it makes bathing children easier, and it can help the elderly to manoeuvre themselves into the bath. The tiles should be non-slip.

OUTDOOR BATHING *left*

An extension is the perfect location for a bathroom, as pipes and drains can be fed easily to the outside. A glazed roof *left* is a neat solution to the problem of introducing daylight while maintaining privacy. Freestanding furniture adds to the airy and spacious atmosphere.

A small rooftop bathroom with an adjacent terrace *above* is about as close as it's possible to get to year-round, open-air bathing.

BATHROOM LAYOUT

Whether you are starting from scratch, or refurbishing an existing bathroom, you probably won't have much choice as to where you position the bathroom fittings. The toilet will need to be placed close to the main waste vent, which is installed when a house is built and is prohibitively expensive to move. And the other fittings have to be placed where they can drain easily into fixed exterior pipes; planning regulations require these to be placed where they are least conspicuous, which is invariably at the back or side of the house, out of sight.

Nevertheless, it is still vital to draw up a scale plan of the room, as this is the only way to work out whether you have enough space to move around and use each fitting. If you are unsure of your draughting skills, use the planning guide enclosed in bathroom fittings brochures. These provide you with squared paper to mark out a room plan, and small cut-out shapes.

In general, you need at least 70cm (28in) of clear floor space in front of the bath or shower to ensure that you can get in or out comfortably, and about 60cm (24in) in front of the toilet and bidet. Sinks need about 70cm (28in) in front to make bending down easier, and at least 15cm (6in) on either side for elbow room. These areas overlap in all but the largest of bathrooms. In a room with low or sloping ceilings, check that you have enough headroom.

A narrow bench can be used as a seat, or to keep clothes and bathrobes off the floor.

Shallow cupboard for extra toiletries.

A pale, fresh colour scheme makes the most of limited daylight.

Storage cupboard.

If more than one member of the household needs to use the bathroom at the same time, it makes sense to visually separate the toilet and bathing areas.

Tiled partitions stop well short of the ceiling to allow daylight to penetrate deeper into the room.

Sink built into worktop, with storage underneath.

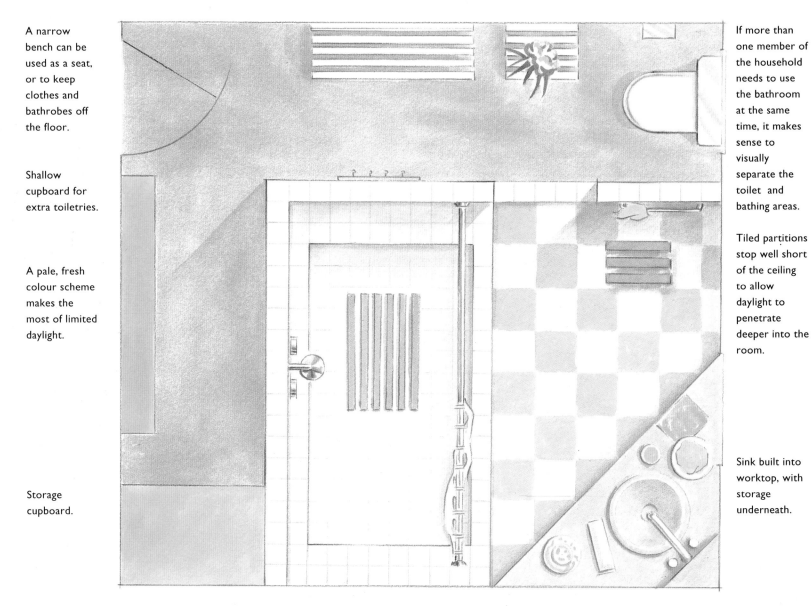

PLAN OF BATHROOM   Tiled shower enclosure is extra large and deep, with drain concealed under slatted wood.

SMALL BATHROOM SOLUTIONS

STRIPED BARE
left

A folding clothes-horse and chair make it easier to move around in a small bathroom, and a wall-mounted sink frees up valuable floor space. Handmade and found objects give the room a welcoming and individual character.

WASHED WOOD
right

Tongue-and-groove panelling makes walls seem warmer than ceramic tiles. Treat it with oil-based paint or shellac to prevent water from penetrating the surface.

Bathrooms in some apartments can be as small as 2.25sq m (24sq ft) in area, so you need to be both economical and creative in your use of space. The traditional approach is to conceal the bath, sink and toilet cistern behind panels. This looks neat and creates extra shelf and cupboard space. Alternatively, sinks and toilets can be wall-hung.

In very small rooms, an inventive approach to space allocation is called for. Scaled-down baths and sinks are readily available, but they can be uncomfortable to use. Where there is no room for a shower tray, let alone a bath, the shower unit can be fixed to the wall – as long as the walls and floor are tiled, or are covered in waterproof material, and there is a drainage hole in the floor. The doorway should have a slightly raised threshold to keep water in the room, and accessories such as towels need to be stored in cupboards to keep them dry.

A shower area which forms part of a bedroom is a good way of creating a second bathroom. It may be possible to fit it into a run of built-in cupboards, or build an enclosure in a corner of the room. The design should ensure that water cannot splash or seep into the room.

STORAGE

- Most items stored in the bathroom are relatively small, and will live happily in cupboards or shelves slotted into narrow spaces or corners.

- If you plan to conceal pipes or fittings behind panels, try to incorporate recessed shelving or cupboards; they look neater and make a better use of the space than wall-mounted furniture.

- The bath, shower and sink all need shelf-space nearby for storing toiletries. Alternatively, use wall-mounted accessories such as sponge holders and soap dishes. Baths can also be organized with a bath rack.

- If the window provides little in the way of light or views, fit glass shelves across the width, and use the space as a storage area.

- Store cosmetics and other small items in trays or boxes, to keep shelves and cupboards neat.

- Use the back of the door for hanging clothes or bathrobes, washbags and a dressing mirror.

- In a high-ceilinged room, a drying rack suspended from the ceiling can be used to store clean towels and linen.

WHITE SPACE

An all-white scheme makes the most of natural light and lends an air of spaciousness. Cupboards under the sink help to organize the many items which need to be stored nearby, while a basket of folded or rolled towels is a practical yet stylish finishing touch.

PRACTICALITIES

GEOMETRIC GLAMOUR *left*

Tiles used on every surface give an awkwardly-shaped bathroom a pulled-together look, and make it easy to clean.

WOODEN BOX *right*

Back-to-wall sinks and toilets help to save space, and concealing ugly pipework behind panels creates a neat finish.

After the kitchen, the bathroom is the most intensively-planned room in the home. In it there are at least three fixed items – and sometimes as many as five or six – all with their own plumbing, drainage and, on occasion, electrical supplies. All the surfaces in the room must be moisture-resistant and attention needs to be paid to comfort factors, such as heat, light and ventilation.

Water pipes and drains are rarely deemed attractive enough to display and are therefore better concealed by wooden panelling, or by running them behind built-in furniture. Toilet cisterns are often given the same treatment. However, access to U-bends and the like should be provided via a door or a removable panel.

Electrical cables and sockets, on the other hand, are concealed or insulated in order to minimize the chances of contact with steam or water. The regulations governing the use of electricity in the bathroom vary from country to country, so check that your plans are safe and legal before making any changes.

Bathrooms can be made safer still by ensuring that both the floor and bath are made from non-slip materials. Hand grips around the bath and shower are worth installing too.

While it makes life easier if all surfaces are tough and easy to clean, there are ways to ensure that the overall look is not hard and clinical. The area around the bath and behind the sink is usually tiled, but it can also be panelled with painted or varnished tongue-and-groove boarding for a softer look, or lined with sheets of safety glass for a dramatic, minimal style. With the exception of wood, virtually any hard flooring material can be laid in here, but for warmth and softness underfoot, choose linoleum or vinyl, seagrass or jute mats, washable rugs or terracotta tiles.

Removing steam and condensation is vital, and all windowless rooms should be fitted with an extractor fan. Keeping the room warm speeds up the process, and obviously makes it more pleasant to use; if the room contains a radiator, consider replacing it with a wall- or floor-mounted towel rail.

MIRRORS AND LIGHTING

- All fittings should be steamproof, as moisture in the air can cause them to short-circuit. Light bulbs must be completely encased in shades, and switches should to be operated with either a pull-cord or located outside the room.

- In a low-ceilinged bathroom, try to use recessed fittings, as this will make the room seem less claustrophobic. It also looks neater.

- Recessed downlighters or spotlights fixed on to the ceiling can be used to provide background light, but try to operate them with a dimmer switch so that their sparkle can be tempered to a soft glow.

- Mirrors used for shaving or applying make up are best lit on either side, as this casts an even, shadow-free light on the face.

- A large mirror creates the illusion of space and can be used by the whole family.

ON DISPLAY

Attractive lights and mirrors help to turn the basin area into a focal point, while cupboards and shelving nearby keep bathroom clutter hidden yet close at hand.

TILING

For sheer variety of size, finish and colour, nothing comes close to ceramic tiles. They offer limitless design possibilities, ranging in size from tiny mosaics to beefy slabs measuring 60cm (24in) or more across, and finishes vary from subtle matt to flashy metallic. Handmade and salvaged tiles create an uneven or rustic look that is worlds away from the smooth finish produced by machine-made tiles. Add to this the possibilities offered by borders, friezes and picture tiles, and you can begin to see why the hardest part of tiling is choosing what to use.

Ceramic tiling is rarely the cheapest way to cover a wall, so it pays to buy exactly the right quantity of tiles to begin with. The easiest way to calculate your requirements is to draw a scale outline of each wall, and the floor if necessary, on squared paper – remember to add windows, radiators and other fixed features.

If you plan to use tiles to create some form of pattern, make a number of photocopies of each drawing beforehand, so you can experiment. A scale drawing makes it easier to see where you might have to cut tiles, usually in corners or around the curves of pipes and fittings. And it tells you how to position them in order to create a balanced look; it's important to use equal-sized tiles on either side of a window, for example. Look closely at examples of tiling in photographs to gain a better idea of how to fit them in awkward areas, such as next to a door frame, or on a window-sill.

Once you have worked out how many tiles are required, add 10 per cent to the quantity if you are using plain tiles, and 20 per cent if using unusually-shaped or patterned tiles. There is always some wastage as a result of breakages and incorrect cutting.

Tile adhesive and grout should both be waterproof if you are tiling wet areas, such as showers or basin splashbacks. Coloured grouts lend interest to plain tiles and blend more easily with handmade or rustic tiles.

LETTERBOX VIEW *above*

Tiling all the surfaces in a bathroom produces a pulled-together look. Brick-shaped tiles echo the shape of the window and appear to 'stretch' the walls, thereby making the room seem bigger.

INSTANT SUNSHINE *right*

A room that is starting to show its age can be given a new lease of life with intense colour. Finishing plain tiles with grout in a contrasting shade helps to break up a large expanse of colour. On the floor, coloured 'slips' enliven a neutral surface.

USING TILES

- If you are feeling confident, tiles can be laid on the diagonal. This kind of design calls for more tiles, as many of them have to be cut up to run the surface up to straight edges or into corners.

- When laid diagonally on a floor, square tiles help to make a small room look larger.

- If you are tiling half-way up a wall, finish the top edge with a row of border tiles. It looks pleasing and stops water from seeping behind the tiles.

- Cheap, machine-made tiles can be made to look more special by mixing them with border or feature tiles in a contrasting colour. You can mix tiles of varying sizes and from different sources as long as they are all the same thickness.

- If the position of bathroom fittings leaves you with an irregularly-shaped floor, lay a border of contrasting tiles a short way from the edges of the room to create a square or rectangular-shaped 'carpet' of colour or pattern. This focusses attention on the centre of the bathroom.

- Handmade, antique and mosaic tiles are often too expensive to be used over a large area, so use them to frame a mirror fixed to the wall, to create a feature above the bath or basin, or to tile splashback areas.

RANDOM ACTS

Terracotta floor tiles cover the walls of a shower with soft, broken colour. Unglazed floor tiles can be used on the walls, but look best if applied by a professional tiler.

Bathroom Accessories

Accessories make a dramatic difference to the style and character of a bathroom and are a good way of introducing contrasts of colour, pattern and texture into a room. Here, where the surfaces are cold and shiny, and fittings are hard and unyielding, it is the accessories which help create a more welcoming feel.

Bathroom clutter tends to collect around the sink and bath, so these are the areas that need most organizing. The essentials are: towel rails or hooks; soap dishes; toothbrush holders; and a shelf where items such as hairbrushes and spectacles can be placed temporarily when you are getting dressed. You also need space for a waste bin, laundry basket, toilet-roll holder, and pots or jars for storing bath salts, cotton wool balls and other toiletries.

Accessories do much to enhance your decorative theme. The rustic overtones of tongue-and-groove panelled walls, for example, can be played up with painted shelves and colourful china, or with galvanized metal and collections of sea shells or pebbles. Clean-cut bathrooms can be glamorized with chrome and glass, or warmed up with baskets and wooden fittings.

CHARACTER PARTS

Baskets and chrome-plated accessories *oposite left* are functional yet stylish additions to a bath area. They organize clutter and dry easily.

All-white fittings set against a pastel-coloured background *opposite right* look sophisticated and somewhat ethereal. The simple lines of the mirrored cabinet and lights give the room a pared-down feel.

left Open shelving and stacked boxes give the same area a more dynamic appearance. The textures of galvanized metal and wood contrast smartly with the smooth white porcelain, and fill the space with warm yet subtle colours.

Scent also furnishes a room; the fresh smell of eucalyptus leaves is released by the steam generated in a hot shower *above*.

FINISHING TOUCHES

SPARKLING EFFICIENCY *left*

Chrome, glass and mosaic turn a small bathroom into a sleekly luxurious retreat. A 'bathroom butler' unit incorporates magnified mirrors, towel rails, shelving and more besides, without cluttering up the wall space.

NAKED DISPLAY *right*

If you have the space, moving the bath away from the wall offers scope for creating floor-to-ceiling storage. Pipework can be concealed behind panels. A stool covered in waffle towelling and displayed objects give this room a lived-in feel.

Like any other room in the house, the bathroom needs a focal point. The window may not be a contender, as it is often rather small, so the job usually falls to the sink or bath areas. Sinks are an obvious focal point, when combined with mirrors and lighting. They can be made to look more imposing by building them into a vanity unit or fitted cupboards, or by forming part of a decorative washstand.

The bath is where we do most of our relaxing, so it makes sense to turn it into a feature in its own right. Instead of squeezing a bath into a corner, give it a greater sense of enclosure by fixing a canopy above, or by flanking it with tall cupboards. In small or low-ceilinged rooms, you may have to content yourself with a raised shelf around the bath, or at each end. It will make the space feel less cramped and provide a resting place for soaps and decorative accessories.

Carefully chosen furniture also makes a good focal point. A colourful freestanding cabinet would be a good contrast to built-in fittings. While a table and chair provides space for displaying flowers and one or two favourite objects, along with piles of towels.

The most suitable soft furnishing fabrics for this room are either soft and absorbent, such as towelling, or those which shrug off water and steam, such as canvas and vinyl. Towelling can be used as a fabric to create a simple window blind or seat cover. Shower curtains made from vinyl are available in an ever-increasing range of colours and designs. Buy two rather than one and hang them at each end of the bath for a more luxurious effect.

All soft furnishings used in a bathroom should be washable. If you plan to trim them with contrast fabrics or braids, use materials which are colourfast and not liable to shrink.

A combination of factors create the right atmosphere in a bathroom, but there are one or two finishing touches which work in every style of room. Lighting candles at bathtime creates a romantic, almost mystical mood; the way reflected flames dance in glass and water becomes hypnotic after a while. And natural scents help to ensure that the air stays sweet and fresh. To aid total relaxation, try using chippings of aromatic woods, such as sandalwood or cedar, bunches of greenery such as eucalyptus or lavender, or place a few drops of essential oil into a vaporizer.

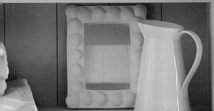

CHILDREN'S BATHROOMS

- Potentially dangerous items, such as medicines, chemicals and scissors, need to be kept away from children, so store them in a lockable box or cabinet.

- When babies are large enough to use the bath, it may have to be fitted with an anti-slip mat.

- A step will enable young children to reach the sink taps.

- Accessories such as toothbrush holders and soap dishes should be made of unbreakable plastics.

- Rugs and mats in the bathroom should be rubber-backed or fitted with anti-slip underlay.

- Bath toys can be stored in a wheeled box or in plastic bins or baskets. Alternatively, fix fabric shoe caddies to the wall, or the back of a door, with pegs.

- It may be worth installing a sink in an older child's room, to relieve pressure on the main bathroom.

JUST FOR KIDS

After safety, cheerful accessories and plenty of toys are the priorities for a trouble-free child bathtime session.

CHAPTER FIVE

CHILDREN'S ROOMS

Children have a tendency to colonize a house, spreading out their belongings over a wide area and commandeering available space for their toys and hobbies and, later on, their friends.

Avoid having to sacrifice your entire house to the next generation by giving them spaces that they can call their own. If you have two living rooms, make one of them a family den, where toys and clutter can gather happily, without interfering with the 'grown-up' area next door.

This chapter shows you how to plan a child's room so that it grows with the child. Specific room plans and dozens of ideas for making the best use of space, furniture and furnishings allow you to cater for your expanding family.

ROOM TO GROW

Children's rooms are different from other parts of the house in one vital respect; the demands made upon them change continually. Babies and children grow out of clothes and toys almost at the same rate as they grow out of furniture and, occasionally, rooms. A nursery is not much fun for an active three year-old with a taste for imaginative play, and the decor you choose for your five year-old may seem babyish well before the age of 10.

Careful planning will help to avoid unnecessary expenditure as your child develops. It may be tempting to give their rooms the 'full' treatment, with themed decor and expensive adornments, but it's worth remembering that children don't need grand paint techniques and complicated murals to structure creative thinking.

Think ahead: if you are making structural alterations, place radiators where they will not impede the arrangement of furniture in a shared room, and install sufficient power sockets so that they can be used later for extra lighting, hi-fis and computers.

The size of your home and family may well dictate that a child's bedroom needs to be shared at some time. As children get older, this compromise will have to be reconciled to their greater need for privacy; adaptable furniture can make life easier. Involving your child in decorating decisions is also a good idea.

RAISED AWARENESS *above*

A high bed-frame frees valuable floor space for a secret hideaway and space for a friend to sleep over. Self-contained bed units create a more integrated look when combined with storage and workspace, while wooden floors and washable rugs are capable of withstanding rough treatment for several years.

PLAY ON COLOUR *right*

Playrooms do not always have to be themed or filled with special equipment. Here, brightly painted market finds and plenty of space are more than enough to spark the imagination.

MAXIMIZING THE SPACE

COSY ATTIC *above*

Children love having big storage boxes full of 'treasure' around them, so think twice before covering up window bays and alcoves with built-in furniture. Store similar-sized toys in the same containers so that large boxes or baskets don't have to be emptied repeatedly in the search for small or lost objects.

TOY PERCH *right*

Low shelving allows toys to be stored at a height where they can be reached easily. Avoid keeping all your child's toys on display as they will quickly lose their novelty value. Hide some away for a few months at a time and swap them over regularly to provide variety.

COLOURED CAMOUFLAGE *left*

A cheerful colour scheme turns an ordinary built-in wardrobe into a vibrant focal point. Basic shelving is painted to match the cupboard, then trimmed with coloured paper. A brightly-painted low table and chair make an attractive place for drawing.

HARD WORK *above*

When space is tight, provide drawing space in the form of low furniture that can be stored neatly against a wall. The area above it can be used for wall-mounted storage and shelving. Wooden drawer units and cardboard magazine files help to keep art materials and papers in order.

Nurseries

In their first few weeks of life, babies need only their parents, food, diapers and a place to sleep, preferably all within close proximity of each other. More than likely, he or she will sleep in your room to begin with.

In time, the baby will move into the nursery, which will eventually become a proper bedroom. If you plan to stay in your house for some years, try not to locate this first bedroom in the smallest room, as it will also be used for work and play as he or she grows older. If the nursery

is tiny, it may be worth thinking about converting an attic or basement at a later date for use as a separate playroom.

To reduce the risk of allergies, dust should be kept to a minimum. Choose either 100 per-cent natural fibres and fabrics for bedlinen and wash new bedding or clothes before use. Avoid using oil-based paints in the nursery, as they continue to release fumes long after the surface has dried. Instead, opt for water-based paints made from natural products.

NURSERY STORE

A changing table with open shelves above allows you to store diapers, stretchsuits, toiletries and the rest of a baby's layette in one convenient spot. A wardrobe fitted with shelves takes care of toys and bulkier clothes.

A new baby can get through several changes of clothing in one day, so hang spare outfits on pegs, or a door-knob *right*. It makes it easier to reach for clean items, gives the baby something bright to focus on, and is often decorative in its own right.

BASIC NURSERY NEEDS

- To create a nursery from scratch you will need:

- A crib, plus crib bumper, mattress, cotton sheets, and wool or other natural-fibre blankets. To avoid danger of suffocation, duvets or pillows should not be used until a child is over one year-old.

- A place to change diapers. You should be able to use this without bending. Keep a basket, shelf or table nearby for storing wipes, diapers, cotton wool and creams.

- A comfortable chair for feeding. It should be possible to sit in it for long periods and to get up easily while holding the baby.

- Storage for clothes and toys. And plenty of it.

- A small basket of toys for when the baby is old enough to sit up and play on the floor.

- A dimmer light, so that you can find your way around the room at night, and a plug-in night light.

- A musical toy for the crib, plus a mobile and posters for the walls. Fix the latter in clip frames so that they can be changed often — babies thrive on variety.

- Depending on the size of your house, a baby alarm or intercom can prove useful.

PLANNING AHEAD

Few people have the budget, or the desire, to redecorate a child's room every three or four years. Instead, changing needs can be met by a cunning adaptation of a few well-chosen basics. A fresh look can be achieved with the help of paint, soft furnishings and accessories.

A room which measures roughly 2.8m x 3.2m (9 x 10½ft) will happily accommodate two children until the eldest is 10 or 11 years old. In the early days of the first child it can be used as a nursery and is best furnished as simply as possible. As shown here, the essentials are: a crib; some adjustable shelving for storing the smaller elements of a baby's layette; a changing area; toy baskets and a comfortable nursing chair.

When the eldest child is roughly 6 years old and the younger child 3, they will need plenty of room to play, so both sleep in a space-saving bunk bed. The shelving unit which was used in the nursery is now devoted to toys storage; in fact, another one was needed to cope with the overflow. Because children love strong colour, a bright red and green scheme was created using a rug and soft furnishings.

As children grow a little older they begin to feel the need for a little independence, so the bunk bed has turned into two separate singles, and the shelving units are repainted to signal their new use as individual workstations. The children chose their own bedlinen and chairs.

THE 3-5 YEAR-OLD'S SHARED ROOM

A bunk bed is fun to sleep on, and keeps other large items of furniture to a minimum.

Scaled-down sofabed for overnight guests.

Drawer boxes under the window are coated with chalkboard paint and used for storing drawing equipment and other small objects.

A flexible layout and furniture which grows with a child are the key to an economical approach to designing and decorating a young person's room

Cluttered shelves are hidden neatly behind a fabric tie-blind.

Peg rails keep shoes, washbags and school knapsacks off the floor.

Tables and benches can be pushed to the wall when they're not in use.

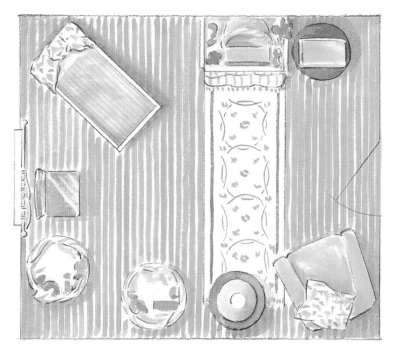

THE NURSERY

Furniture for the nursery should be chosen with a view to possible future use. A sturdy crib can be passed on to relatives or friends when it is no longer needed; the other furniture can be used elsewhere.

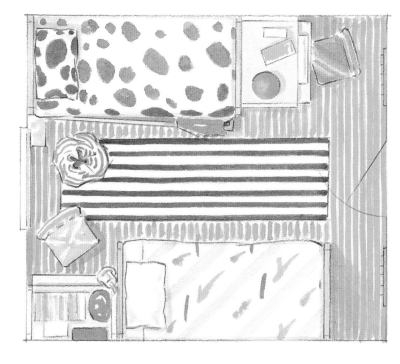

OLDER CHILDREN'S ROOM

Single beds and individual work areas give each child a degree of privacy and independence. Storage boxes keep clutter under control.

SAFETY

- Check that any furniture used in children's rooms conforms to local safety regulations, even if it is second-hand or inherited. Any paints or varnishes used on walls and floors should be eco-friendly.

- Buy safety gates for stairs. Avoid pressure-mounted designs — they can give way.

- Avoid placing furniture under a window, as it makes it easier for a toddler to climb onto the windowsill. Logic dictates that all windows, and some doors, should be fitted with safety locks.

- All children's rooms should be fitted with a smoke alarm. Check them regularly to see that they are still working.

- Fit unused power sockets with safety covers and always avoid trailing cords.

- Keep all medicines in a lockable cabinet.

- Never buy cabinets or cupboards which have child-height glass doors and avoid buying furniture with tall or spindly legs, which can topple over too easily.

WORK, REST AND PLAY

Children appreciate a certain amount of order in their rooms, so encourage them to share in the tidying up as well as the more pleasurable task of displaying favourite items.

DECORATING A NURSERY

Decorating a nursery is the time-honoured way of preparing for the arrival of a new baby. The temptation to go overboard can be overwhelming, especially as family and friends use this time to shower you with gifts and hand-me-downs. However, it's worth remembering that baby-hood is a comparatively short period of time; before you buy an expensive item of equipment or furniture, ask yourself how long you are likely to need it, and whether it can be adapted for other uses. Thinking ahead helps reduce unnecessary expenditure.

It is best to decorate a nursery so that it can be updated easily after a few years. Painted walls are preferable to wallpaper, as they are quicker to change, and can be touched up if scuffed. The floor covering needs to be comfortable, warm, easily cleaned and durable. Cushioned vinyl, linoleum, wood and cork are all suitable.

It also helps to choose a window treatment that blocks out the light efficiently, both to avoid problems with early waking or reluctance to sleep on summer evenings, and to dim the room during daytime naps. This need not mean using dark curtains or blinds, which can make a room gloomy; special blackout blinds or lined curtains can be used instead. Since many babies can crawl after just a few months, avoid floor and table lamps – ceiling and wall lights are much safer options.

Furniture needs to be safe, comfortable, functional and adaptable. A crib is the only essential item of furniture made solely for babies, so choose one which is generously proportioned and solidly built; it can then be used until your first child is about two years old, and subsequently by younger siblings.

You also need a place for changing diapers. This can take the form of a changing mat laid across the top of a chest of drawers or a purpose-made changing table. Any flat, stable and reasonably deep surface will do, as long as you can clean and change the baby without bending.

ALL LINED UP *above*

Laundry baskets lined with a large square of fabric make cheap and effective toy stores. Hem the fabric edges to prevent fraying.

SIMPLY CHARMING *right*

Creating a cheerful and stimulating nursery is rarely a matter of filling it with coordinated furnishings. Simple wall and window treatments, and furniture that will evolve to suit a child's changing needs, work just as well.

A Shared Bedroom

Younger children often enjoy the companionship that results from sharing a room, but they do need enough space to move around. When one of them reaches school age, he or she needs to be able to pursue individual interests. You can make this easier by providing a work and a play surface for each child. Alternatively, create several loosely-defined activity areas in the room: for example, a book corner with miniature chairs or a sofa and a basket of books; an art area with an easel and chalkboards; or a home corner with a play house.

Creating room to move will mean freeing up additional floor space, so bunk beds are a practical solution. It is often recommended that children should not sleep more than 80cm (31in) above the floor until they are over six years old, but many are perfectly able to make the psychological adjustment at a younger age. If in doubt, buy a bunk bed which can convert to two singles. In any event, the top bunk should be fitted with a safety rail, and the gap between any two rails should be no more than 7.5cm (3in) wide.

From pre-school-age onwards, children bring home a steady stream of pictures and models, and their room is an obvious place to display a favourite selection. Place them low on the walls, at their eye level. This is also the age when children often develop an interest in collecting, so try to provide space for a rapidly growing set of dinosaurs, car stickers or dolls' accessories. Low shelves and window-sills can be used to show off precious models.

At some time or other, most children scribble on the walls, either by accident or on purpose, so make sure the surfaces are scrubbable and easily retouched. The bedroom is also likely to be used as a home gym – beds make splendid trampolines, especially if you jump with a friend, and shelving units can be treated like climbing frames – the furniture must be sturdy and stable enough to take a hammering. And adjustable shelves should be locked into position.

PLAYTIME

Colourful bedlinen and pictures look great against soft, neutral walls *top*. Lights in a young child's room should always be fitted with safety grilles.

To keep your child's artistic endeavours off the walls, paint plywood boxes with chalkboard paint *above* and fix them at an accessible height.

right Children respond well to strong colour in their surroundings – primary colours are stimulating, and green is particularly restful.

USING FABRIC

Easy-care bedlinen and window treatments are a necessity in children's rooms. If hard flooring is used, cover it with one or two cotton rugs to make for softer landings. Fabric-covered crib canopies and bumpers look wonderfully pretty, are cheap to buy or make, and can be put away or passed on when no longer needed. Patchwork quilts and cushions are perfect for children's rooms and while they can be delicate, children do learn to look after beautiful things in time. Sturdy and washable fabrics, such as canvas, towelling and hessian are useful for making toy-storage and wash bags.

In smaller children's rooms, curtains are best made to window-sill height, as the temptation to pull constantly at floor-length drapes is irresistible. In an older child's room, curtains should not be so long that there is a danger of tripping over them. Curtains can also be used as screening: try hanging long drapes from a ceiling-fixed track or pole, to give the occupants of a shared room a degree of privacy. Or hang them in a traditional box bed to keep out draughts and create a greater sense of enclosure.

Here, colourful striped cotton is used to make a simple covering for freestanding shelving. Clutter can easily be hidden from view, while making it easy for children to retrieve items from the lower shelves. Fabric panels added to each side of the unit would make it look more like a wardrobe.

MATERIALS

Fabric

Pins

Eyelet pack

Hammer

Pencil

Rope

Screw-in cup hooks

1 CUTTING THE FABRIC

Take a length of fabric, 100cm (40in) wide and 180cm (70in) long. Allow a seam allowance of 6cm (2½in) at either side and at the bottom, and 7.5cm (3in) along the top edge. Turn under raw edges, pin, then machine-hem all four sides.

2 ATTACHING EYELETS

Take your fabric and measure 3.5cm (1½in) down from the top and 3.5cm (1½in) in from the edge. Mark this point with a pencil. Repeat for each corner of the panel then insert the eyelets from the pack and hammer them in position.

3 HANGING THE BLIND

Mark the positions of the cup hooks with a pencil at the top of the unit. Screw in cup hooks. Slip the top set of eyelets over the hooks. Loop the fabric blind upwards and place the bottom eyelets over the hooks as well.

4 TIEING THE BLIND

To secure the blind, cut two lengths of 1cm- (½in-) diameter rope, each twice the length of the blind plus 12cm (4in). Fix two cup hooks to the top of the unit and loop the pieces of rope over them. Gently roll up the blind according to preference and tie the two ends of rope in a bow at the bottom.

STORAGE IDEAS

- Sturdy bookcases are highly adaptable: they can be used to store diapers and clothes in the nursery; books and toys as the children grow, and hi-fis when they reach adolescence. Choose a design with adjustable shelves and a finish that can be painted over.

- Chests of drawers can store a wide variety of items. Drawer pulls should be large enough for older children to grab easily.

- Choose a wardrobe with an adjustable hanging rail, so that it can be raised progressively as the child grows older.

- Fix wall-mounted shelves with uprights and brackets for maximum flexibility. When cut to fit exactly, they make better use of an alcove or recess than freestanding furniture. If a hanging rail is mounted to the underside of the lowest shelf, it can also be used for storing clothes.

- Use storage drawers on runners or castors under the beds.

- A toy box or blanket chest can be used to store large toys. Lidded boxes can double as a drawing surface, since children will happily kneel down to play. Stacking boxes make better use of limited floor space, and some can be fitted with wheels.

- Baskets are pretty, and it's easy to find uses for them elsewhere in the home.

- Use pegs to hang clothes and bags on the wall, or behind a door.

OLDER CHILDREN

THREE YEARS ON...

Painted shelving *left* creates a combined storage and work area. Clip-on fittings can be used to light a desktop, but these should not be fixed to a bed frame or near soft furnishings.

right Tall storage can be used to give each child a greater feeling of privacy, but it's best not to use bulky items, as these can make the room gloomy. A storage box under the bed is a good place to store sports equipment, while noticeboards allow you to deal with a succession of fads and collecting passions.

School gradually alters the way children use their rooms. They will need a quiet place to do their homework, especially after spending all day and perhaps part of the evening in the company of other children. And extra space will need to be found for their latest fad, be it a sudden interest in fashionable clothes or a mania for collecting plastic insects.

In a shared room, make sure each child has his or her own work area in order to pursue individual activities. Arrange the desks or tables so that they face away from each other to increase the feeling of privacy. Lights should be directable, as in any other work area, and each child should have their own reading light, so that one can sleep while the other reads.

Extra hanging space for clothes and more shelving for books and collections will be necessary, although a regular clear-out will improve matters slightly. It's often possible to add to modular storage; if the room is furnished with freestanding items, this would be a good time to add built-in shelving.

A ROOM OF YOUR OWN

There comes a time when sharing a room ceases to be a viable proposition, especially for a boy and girl. When this happens, you may have no alternative but to rethink the layout of your home. Structural work may be necessary, to expand into the attic or to build an extension perhaps. Or you may be able to get away with dividing a large room into two with tall bookcases. The way you decorate and furnish the new spaces will need to change too: the look can be more grown-up, and it's okay to choose materials that require slightly more care and maintenance, such as carpeting and wallpaper.

If your child has been sleeping in the same bed since the age of two or three, it could well be time for a new frame and mattress too.

PERSONAL SPACE *above*

A bed frame with built-in drawers and a dresser unit provide a sensible mix of storage and display space. Children like to hide things away, so provide an area for personal belongings as well as clothes.

A SHARED DEN

A room dedicated to play and entertainment is a good idea, especially if the children's bedrooms are small. Large favourite toys and space-consuming hobbies can be sited here, without the repeated necessity for them to be cleared up to make way for other activities. This is also a good place for the television and computer if you want to keep the living area looking reasonably grown-up and formal.

The subject of shared play space requires careful handling, as younger children often go through a stage of wanting to take part in their older siblings' activities. To maintain harmony, it's worth giving older children a work or play surface that youngsters cannot reach easily.

ACTIVITY CENTRE *above*

In a playroom, floors are collecting points for food, drinks, glue, paint and outdoor dirt, so they need to be easy-to-clean. Storage can take many forms, but it may be worth having high-level shelves or a tall cupboard, to keep some toys out of the reach of younger children.

01/01/80 00:16   Directory B:*.*
Document Size: 0   Free Disk Space: 172032

   . <CURRENT>   <DIR> | .. <PARENT>   <DIR>
   ALEXON. .   <DIR> 01/01/80 01:42 | ALFAROME.EST   1872 01/01/80 00:47

CHAPTER SIX

WORKSPACES

Make working from home a pleasure, whether it is a full-time occupation or a couple of hours a week spent doing administration at the kitchen table.

Choose the right site for your workspace to begin with, then concentrate on creating a sense of privacy, as well as providing supportive seating, generous storage and efficient lighting. If you have the space, consider whether you could use this room for relaxing too. Also, remember that it's okay to personalize it with colour, humour and favourite possessions. If you're proud of your work, show it.

INSPIRING WORKSPACES

BELOW STAIRS *left*

The wasted space under stairs can easily be turned into a compact office, as long as both the worksurface and storage areas are clearly lit. A corner leg lends extra support to a deep cantilevered shelf, used as a table top.

LIGHT WORK *right*

Plenty of daylight and a pleasant view always make working more of a pleasure. Here, a glass-topped trestle table and metal drawer cabinet provide a stylish yet low-cost alternative to the conventional office desk, while miniature tin trunks help to keep a pigeon-hole filing system under control.

A home office should be more than just the room or corner where you earn your living or pay the bills. Like a bedroom, it is often a private or solitary space; a spot where you can be yourself, and plan, make decisions or dream. Working and living under one roof offers many advantages: it frees you from the tedium of commuting and office politics, and allows you to choose your own hours; but it also blurs the necessary divisions between work and leisure. For this reason, it's important to separate your workspace from the rest of your home.

The minimum requirements in any workspace are: a surface to work at, a chair to sit on, stor-

age, and light. Even where writing or using the telephone are the main activities, the surface only needs to be level, at a height that allows you to tuck your knees underneath, and stable – especially if it supports heavy computer equipment. A farmhouse-style kitchen table, or a deep shelf cantilevered off the wall would work just as well.

You cannot afford to be as quixotic in your choice of chair. As well as supporting your spine, a chair should allow you to sit at the correct height relative to the worksurface, it should swivel and glide easily along the floor if you regularly need access to storage nearby, and tuck

neatly under the table when not in use. Few domestic chairs do the job as well as those designed for office use, and you may have to sacrifice aesthetics for the sake of your posture.

If you have the space, include an easy chair or a sofa so you can take a break every so often without having to venture too far. When your concentration begins to slip, it helps to rest for ten minutes or so.

Well-planned storage not only organizes your papers and accessories, it also does much to create a better working atmosphere; closing a cabinet door or drawer on working clutter can help you to move onto the next task.

SITING A WORKSPACE

When choosing where to work, look for a room which is quiet, and well away from household activity and diversions. Try to avoid placing a workspace near playrooms, kitchens or other communal areas. It also helps if the room gets plenty of light, although you may want to reserve the sunniest room in the house for living and relaxing. If you have co-workers or regular visitors, place your work area where a path to the office doesn't necessitate a guided tour of the house.

A separate office is much the best option, as it allows you to psychologically distance yourself by shutting the door. And it may be worth rearranging the layout of your home to create a specific room, especially if you work full-time.

DOMESTIC WORK

above Plenty of even and shadow-free light makes drawing and painting even more of a pleasure in a high-level studio.

right In a multi-purpose space, siting computer and home entertainment equipment next to one another makes cable management easier.

ARRANGING FURNITURE

- Office furniture can be arranged galley-style, just like a kitchen, with a desk in front of you, and storage behind. This works well in open-plan rooms, where one of the elements can act as an island unit.

- In boxy spaces, try creating an L-shape using a table, and either a low filing cabinet or computer table placed at one side and set at right angles.

- A single line of units may be the most sensible arrangement in a narrow room, but don't forget to make the most of the wall space with shelving.

- A room with a view is a great asset, but it can also be a distraction. You may prefer to face the wall, or into the room, when it's necessary to concentrate on the job in hand.

- Computer screens should not be placed in front of, or facing, a light source or window. They are best lit from one side.

- In shared workspaces, try to give each person his or her own storage space.

- Versatility is the key to arranging workspaces in multi-purpose rooms. Use storage cabinets on castors so they can be wheeled out of sight. Or build equipment into a cupboard so that it can be hidden away.

- If you're not a slave to new technology, a bureau or rolltop desk also hides working clutter quickly and easily.

LIGHT WORK

Being able to work in a conservatory is only a dream for many people. A fabric awning cuts down glare around the computer screen.

GET ORGANIZED

Even the smallest workspace often needs to accommodate a wide variety of literature, tools and accessories. If you make a list of the items which you use regularly, it might well include: writing or drawing instruments; paper and other stationery in a multitude of shapes and sizes; the telephone and answer machine; several pieces of computer equipment; a desk-lamp; filing trays; books, journals and correspondence; not to mention desk toys, holiday souvenirs and personal mementoes. Most of us simply wouldn't be able to function unless the space was organized in some way.

Your storage system should ensure that the most frequently-used items are easiest to reach,

preferably without getting up from your chair. If you are driven mad by clutter, you need a system which allows you to store as much as possible behind closed doors. For the sake of visual neatness, opt for built-in cupboards or shelving concealed behind blinds, rather than a mish-mash of filing cabinets or an old wardrobe.

On the other hand, you may be the type who uses your desk as a horizontal filing cabinet, with 'to do' piles and scattered notes serving as reminders of the day's tasks. A large desk which allows you to spread out is your greatest priority, and, if you abide by the classic storage principle of 'divide and rule' it need not lead to even greater chaos. This means storing items in small

groups, so they are easy to see and retrieve. You might, for example, keep separate containers for each type of pen and pencil, or use a pegboard to organize smaller items of office equipment, rather than throwing everything into one drawer.

Electronic storage, in the form of computer information software, can help to reduce the amount of storage space needed, but some form of filing system is still a necessity in most offices, even if it's only used for storing bills. It may be that the classic filing cabinet, with its vertically-hung files, meets your needs best; as a rule of thumb, you need twice as much storage as you think you do, so buy a four-drawer

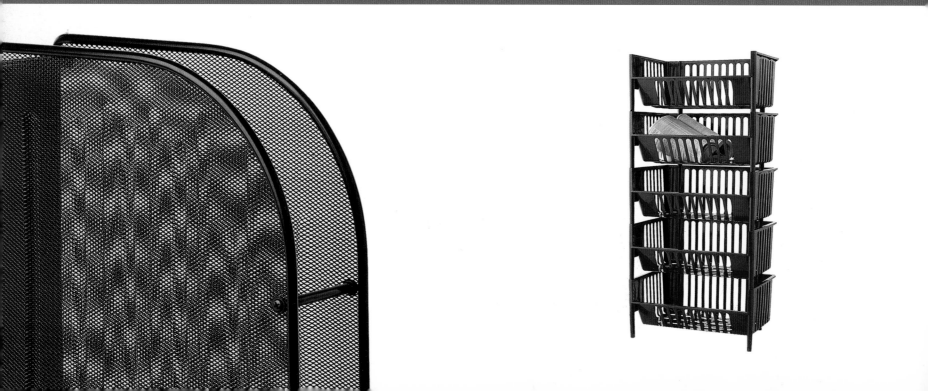

rather than a two-drawer model; after all, it takes up no more floor space.

If you need to be able to see what files contain at a glance, or store swatches and samples, box or magazine files stored on shelves may suit you better, although they take up more floor space. A prettier way of achieving the same result is to store items in baskets or decorated boxes. In addition, a tower of stacking vegetable baskets can be used to keep work in progress off the desk top, yet close at hand.

The secret of organizing the desktop is to avoid covering the entire surface. This applies to computer equipment as much as anything else: even people who think they spend all day at the keyboard need somewhere to set down papers and the morning mail.

The best desk accessories are not always those designed specifically for the purpose. Small cabinets which are meant for storing nails and screws are equally useful for storing.paper clips and other small items of stationery; pen holders can be fashioned from flower pots, small vases or chemistry beakers; and a sturdy spring will hold business cards and scraps of paper in a stylish manner.

Good organization also means keeping waste to a minimum. Use generous-sized bins or baskets to collect and sort paper for recycling, and use recycled paper products.

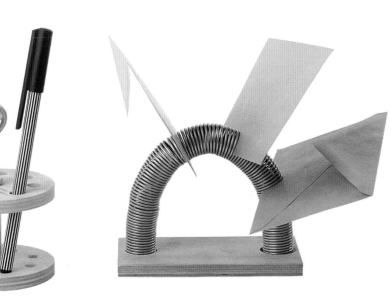

PRACTICALITIES

Whatever you use your workspace for – be it writing or woodwork, sculpture or sewing – it needs to be furnished for comfort and practicality. When necessary, it should be easy to change the mood from bright and business-like to calm and relaxing. And it needs to be good for your health, especially if you spend large amounts of time there.

Unless you work standing up, your priority is to ensure that all parts of your body are cor-rectly supported when you sit at your desk or table. Poor posture can leave you feeling unwell and create serious health problems over time. It can also adversely affect your productivity.

Your first step should be to choose the right chair. It needs to be adjustable in height, with a curved back to support your lower spine. Ideally, the back should also be wide and high enough to support your shoulders and head, with armrests to take the weight off your neck

BACK TO BASICS

In a workspace, a stylish coordinated look is less important than a set-up which enables you to work happily and efficiently. Most of your needs can be met by good natural light and basic but sturdy furniture *above*.

A surface which is used for sewing or other close work *right* needs to be slightly lower than standard desk height, ideally about 66cm (26in) high. A task lamp suspended just above the table casts a bright and shadow-free light.

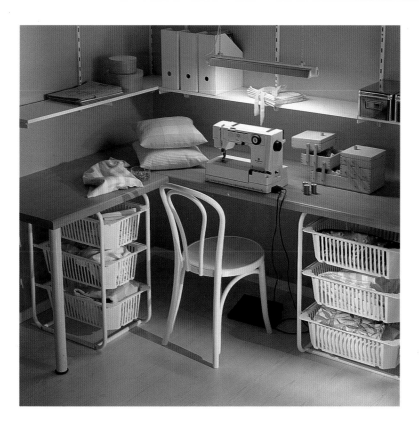

ELECTRONIC AND TELECOMMUNICATIONS EQUIPMENT

- Do you need additional telephone lines for the fax, modem, and other business equipment and services?

- Do you have enough power sockets to run all the items of electronic equipment?

- Keep computers away from direct sunlight, and leave enough space around each box for the cooling fans to operate efficiently.

- Both hard disk drives and floppy disks should be kept away from devices that create strong magnetic fields, such as transformers or electric motors.

- Consider fitting a surge protector to power sockets which are used to operate computers and modems.

- Photocopiers give off unpleasant fumes, and sometimes carbon monoxide. If you have one in your home, store it outside your workspace, in a ventilated area.

- Electrical equipment dehumidifies the air and gives it a positive electrical charge, both of which contribute to an unhealthy working atmosphere. Houseplants and an ionizer can help to counteract this.

FUNCTIONAL COLOUR

A coat of paint gives trestle tables and shelving a unified look, while plants and a green colour scheme help to create a healthy atmosphere.

and shoulders. When sitting in the chair, your feet should rest flat on the floor, with your knees very slightly lower than your hips. And it should be possible to rest your hands on the keyboard or table top, with your arms relaxed by your sides, and your elbows bent at 90 degrees.

To minimize neck pain and eye strain when using a computer, place the top of the screen roughly level with your forehead, and 45-50cm (18-20in) from your face. If you use the computer for long periods, treat yourself to a padded wrist rest for your mouse or keyboard, and make sure you get up and move around every 30 minutes or so – more often if you have breathing or postural problems.

It is worth buying a computer desk so you position the keyboard and monitor at the right height. But it's best not to make this your only work-surface, as most tailor-made models are too small to accommodate paper-work as well as hardware. If you are on a tight budget, consider placing a rigid surface on top of a couple of low filing cabinets. This works almost as well, because their height comes fairly close to that required for a computer or typewriter table, between 66-74cm (26-30in) high.

As in all activity areas, good background and task lighting is critical. The former can be provided with a wall- or floor-mounted uplighter, as long as the ceiling is not painted a dark colour; pendant fittings and fluorescent bulbs are best avoided, as they cause glare, which soon becomes tiring. Most types of task light sit on the worksurface, but it is possible to buy wall-mounted fittings if you are short of space.

TEMPORARY WORKSPACES

EASILY DRAWN

A designer's drawing board sits on a lightweight frame to blend more easily into a living space. Working at home frees you to create your own tailor-made filing systems.

Traditionally, celebrated writers saw no need for a separate office. Many penned their words wherever they felt most inspired – even if this happened to be in bed. As we now live in the age of the laptop computer and electronic personal organizers, you could even argue that tables and, to some extent, chairs are no longer a necessity. However, most of us are rather conventional in this respect, and still prefer to work in a room or a corner that looks the part.

The most popular places to site a temporary workspace are the bedroom and kitchen. As the bedroom gets only part-time use, working here makes better use of the space, but care needs to be taken to ensure that the two activities remain distinct from one another. Working clutter, and the effects of electrical equipment on air quality, do not make for a healthy sleeping atmosphere. During the day, the temptation to take a nap may be overwhelming.

As the bed usually dominates the room, the answer may be to turn your back on it, perhaps by siting the workspace under a window. However, the room should be considered as a whole when deciding on decor and furnishings: a very cosy or girlish scheme will grate on the senses when you're trying to work, as will an executive-style desk when it's time to relax.

The kitchen may be a more suitable location for temporary working, as it is more likely to be planned for business-like activity. However, the rest of the household will need to be taught to congregate elsewhere, and it soon becomes irritating to have to clear up at the end of every working period. On the other hand, you may prefer to be surrounded by bustle and activity.

It can seem like a good idea to site a work area in the living room but it may not work in practice as, once again, it can be hard to separate work from relaxation. Choosing the right floor covering can also be tricky: a hardwearing surface is needed to withstand the punishment meted out by constantly moving furniture. Wood and other hard floors are usually durable enough, but rugs and some types of natural floorcovering snag easily in furniture castors.

More unconventional locations for a workspace include circulation areas, such as a hallway or landing. If you can't find space inside the house, the ideal spot may be a shed or a greenhouse at the end of the garden, as long as you can provide it with a safe electrical supply for light, and a heat source for when it gets colder.

If the workspace, or the room in which it is situated, is likely to be used by others, it should reflect their needs too. A height-adjustable chair, and storage that they can call their own, makes life easier for older children. If there are young children about, unused power sockets should be fitted with safety covers, there should be no trailing cords, sharp corners on furniture may have to be rounded off, and small objects will need to be stored in a childproof drawer. Remember also that young children love copying their parents: it may be worth keeping scrap paper and pens nearby for the times when they want to play at 'working'. Also, make sure any valuable data on your computer is secure.

If you have a separate office which only gets infrequent use, try combining it with other part-time activities, such as playing music or exercise. If the room is likely to be noisy, it's a good idea to fix sound-proofing materials to the walls and floor, and perhaps double glaze the windows. Using the space as a spare bedroom is much easier, as the only extra furnishings needed are a sofa bed, and perhaps a blanket box for storing linen.

WORKING WARDROBE *left*

In a bedroom, the problem of how to hide the workspace has been solved by building it into the wardrobes. Part of the workstation can be pulled into the room, to minimize any feelings of claustrophobia.

VIRTUAL OFFICE *above*

A portable computer makes it possible to work virtually anywhere. Dining rooms make good temporary workspaces, as they are seldom in constant use. In any multi-purpose space, matters can be improved by screening off the work area, perhaps with a folding screen.

CHAPTER SEVEN

HALLWAYS

A warm welcome and a hint of what's to come are all you need to create the perfect hall. Forego bulky furniture in favour of space-efficient storage and generous helpings of colour, texture and dramatic display.

As well as choosing surface finishes that wear well and prevent outdoor dirt from travelling any further, make a statement with bold displays of favourite photographs and pictures, flattering lighting, and by highlighting architectural features, such as windows and staircases. Create intriguing vistas into adjacent rooms. And look afresh at 'dead' spaces such as stair cupboards and landings: there is often potential for turning them into work or play areas.

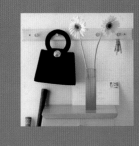

FIRST IMPRESSIONS COUNT

ON THE SHELF
far left

A pale and neutral colour scheme, recessed shelves and mirror tiles maximize the sense of space in a boxy hallway. Decorative interest is added with a colourful poster.

OUTDOOR GEAR *below left*

A neat display of hats and coats adds charm, but may not be suited to very narrow spaces. However, room could be found almost anywhere for this elegant wicker umbrella stand.

SHOE STORE *left*

A hall cabinet provides a good mix of display and storage space, especially if the interior can be fitted out with shelves.

Although a hall or lobby is usually the first space you see when entering a home, it is often the last to receive any decorative consideration; priority tends to be given to 'proper' rooms, such as the living area or kitchen. However, a hallway serves symbolic as well as practical purposes: it creates a buffer zone between the outside and the rest of your home; a place where you can begin to let down your guard. It needs to feel welcoming and serve as a visual introduction to the rest of your home.

Any evaluation of the space should begin at the front door, as creating the right impression has a lot to do with making it feel secure. Doors with large areas of glass let the light in, and make it easier to see who is outside, but they also make the room feel more exposed. If the door is made from thin panels fixed to a soft-wood frame, it is unlikely to offer much resistance to potential intruders, so reinforce it, or better still, replace it with a solid hardwood door. Glazed panels in a door may have to be fitted with laminated glass or iron grilles.

As a hallway is likely to be small, it needs to be kept free of clutter. Coats should be hung where they cannot impede full opening of the front door, or block your passage. A small table or shelf near the door is useful for leaving messages or the mail. Like any other room, halls need a focal point too. As floor space is likely to be at a premium, create areas of interest with pictures and other wall-mounted displays.

CHECKERED ENTRANCE

A porch provides
useful shelter as well
as extra security, and a
doormat helps to keep
dirt and wet out of the
house. When a space
has several doors
opening off it, try to
direct attention on to
the floor.

Making a Statement

As we pass through halls and lobbies fairly quickly, it seems somehow appropriate to make a bold statement with the decor and furnishings. This need not be difficult: a dramatic colour for the walls, or a well-placed mirror, may be all you need to give it strength of character.

In older houses especially, the staircase is the most obvious feature of a hallway. It may not sweep dramatically upwards, Hollywood style, but it is unlikely to be an eyesore either, so it's worth giving it due prominence, perhaps by painting it in a contrasting colour, or by installing a different floor treatment. This has practical advantages too: bare stairs can be noisy, and dangerous if highly polished, so are best covered with carpet or a fixed runner.

Look also at the vistas created as you look from the hall into other rooms. Painting the hall so that it harmonizes with the spaces beyond, or carefully placing an object at the end of the vista to create a focal point, will link the hall more firmly with the rest of your home.

It may be necessary to improve the proportions of the space, particularly if it is narrow or high-ceilinged. An expanse of mirror is the classic way to widen and brighten up a small space.

Unless you're blessed with plenty of space, cupboards and other conventional forms of storage in a hallway are likely to create an obstruction. It may be possible to find room for a narrow cabinet or table with shelves or pegs above; or you could combine seating and storage in a narrow bench. When used in conjunction with a group of pictures, a decorative mirror, or a small display of objects on a tabletop, make attractive focal points.

Lastly, remember that good light is by far the most effective way to liven up a hall. A row of sparkling spotlights or wall-mounted uplighters can lead you into the house, while directable fittings are more appropriate if you want to focus attention on pictures. The staircase should be lit for safety, and it should be possible to distinguish clearly between the treads and risers.

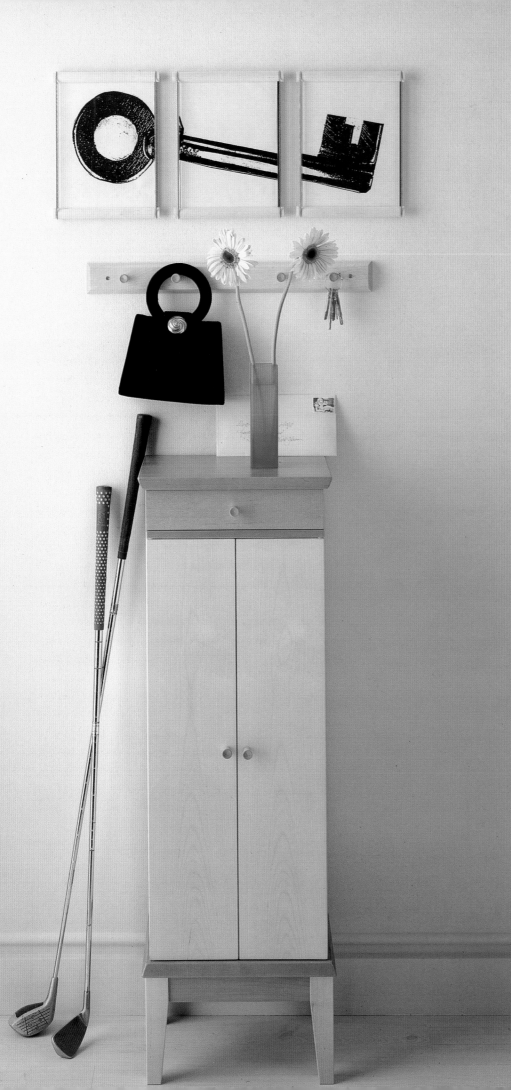

ON THE SURFACE

opposite Scaled-down furniture for hallways doesn't have to be shy and retiring: here, a curvaceous console table and a circular mirror help to soften a stark and rectilinear space.

left The need for somewhere to deposit keys and other personal items needs to be weighed against the fact that horizontal surfaces accumulate clutter at an alarming rate in the hall. A tall and narrow cabinet, combined with a peg rail, ingeniously resolves the dilemma. A greatly enlarged photocopy of a key is strikingly displayed in a trio of frames.

above Chunky square picture frames create a light-hearted contrast to a delicate console table.

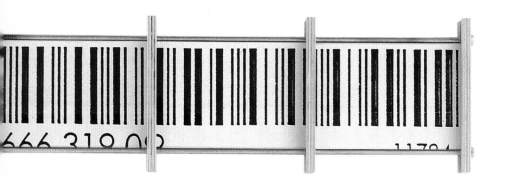

DISPLAYING PICTURES

As halls and lobbies need to be kept free of obstructions, they are ideal places to display pictures. Your choice of pictures will greatly affect how you perceive and feel about the space. And the way you hang and frame them largely determines whether they will be enjoyed and appreciated, or merely tolerated.

Choosing pictures is one of the nicest parts of creating a home, but it's not something you can do by adhering to fixed rules. While themed groups and sets of prints are an easy way to create a harmonious display, eclectic collections of images that you love are also certain to work together. 'Art' can take the form of anything; from postcards and found objects to looped string and old textile fragments. Your favourite pieces need not even hang in the conventional way: casually propping a picture on a shelf or table, or displaying postcards in clips hung from hooks, looks less precious and makes it easy to rearrange the space.

Buying a picture because it matches the colour of your walls is usually a mistake. If you are worried that a picture may not 'go' in the room, choose a mount and a frame that visually links the image with the walls. Sometimes a single bold image against an otherwise bare wall can make more of a dramatic statement than a collection of small images.

Frame styles range from ornate to almost-invisible, and as a rule, they should focus your attention on the image, rather than detract from it. For example, a colourful print can be made to look even more cheerful by placing it in a frame that picks out one of the colours in the image. While the simplicity of a graphic black-and-white image is often enhanced by a border-less clip frame. Traditional pictures are usually given a striking gilt or metallic frame to make them look brighter.

The size of the frame also matters. Most images need space to breathe, so there should be a gap between the edge of a picture and the inner edge of the frame. This is known as the mount. It is often coloured to make the picture

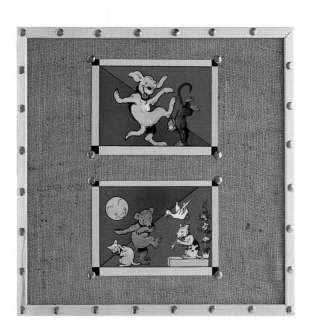

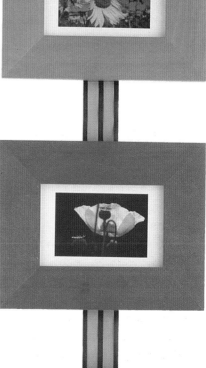

look bigger, or exaggerated in scale to make a small image look more important. It's also worth experimenting with the depth of the frame, as this can help to give simple images a more arresting appearance.

Another good way to liven up a picture is to customize the surround. Thumb tacks can be pushed straight into softwood for a studded look, while a wide range of objects, from buttons to twigs, can be stuck directly onto a basic frame using a multi-purpose adhesive. If you're feeling dextrous, you could even cover it with paper or fabric.

The most commonly made mistake when hanging pictures is to scatter them around a wall, so that each one struggles to make an impression. Like other finishing touches, small- and medium-sized pictures look best in a group. An identically-framed set or similar pairs can be arranged in a straight line, or symmetrically; but a mixed group looks better when it forms an asymmetric shape on the wall. Experiment with possible arrangements by laying the pictures out on the floor. When creating an asymmetrical arrangement, hang the largest picture first.

Take care not to place pictures too high, where they will not be seen easily. As halls are often narrow, remember to place larger pictures at the end of the space, rather than ranging them along the side walls.

WALLS, FLOORS AND STAIRCASES

Hall surfaces need to be extremely durable. The constant movement of people and possessions between the inside and outside, and from one room to another, make it foolhardy to use flimsy or delicate wall and floor treatments here. And as the space is often awkwardly-shaped, with lots of doors thrown in for good measure, the surfaces should unify the space.

Rain and outdoor grime is continually brought into the house via the front door, so a large doormat is a must, and the floor needs to be easy to sweep or wipe clean. Ceramic tiles, brick, wood and stone are all ideal, and can always be combined with a washable runner if you feel the look is too hard, or needs colour. A runner will also soften heavy foot-falls and keep fitted carpets clean. All loose rugs should be fitted with an anti-slip underlay.

If the same flooring material is used here and in adjoining rooms, the spaces will seem to flow easily into one another. Changing the floor treatment has the opposite effect, and makes them feel more separate; it is often done in an open-plan space to give the living area a greater sense of enclosure.

In small or narrow areas, the lower parts of the walls are also likely to get considerable wear and tear. Shopping bags and bicycles will regularly scrape past, and when furniture is moved around, it is bound to cause dents and scratches. The answer may be to divide the wall horizontally, with a tough treatment, such as tongue-and-groove panelling or textured wallpaper, used below; while a cheaper and less durable finish, such as paint, is applied above. A narrow shelf or wooden rail helps to hide the joins where the two meet, and so creates a neater finish. Dividing the wall in this way can also make a narrow space seem wider.

Lastly, make sure the staircase is safe to use. There should always be a hand rail on one side, and balustrading if it has an open construction. Leave the treads bare only if they are made from a non-slip material. Otherwise, they should be covered with fitted carpet, or a fixed runner. Open treads can be covered with textured rubber sheeting, or, alternatively, fitted with anti-slip strips.

Consider also whether you could make better use of the space around the stairs. It may be possible to open up the area underneath, to make space for a study, laundry facilities, or a children's play area. Or place an easy chair on a wide landing to create a reading corner.

CONTROLLED ENTRY *below left*

A simply furnished lobby echoes the restful mood of an adjoining living area. Wooden flooring used throughout maximizes the sense of space.

PANELLED WALK *below centre*

Tongue-and-groove panelling in a corridor is extended into the rooms beyond to blur the divisions between circulation and living space. Alcoves are usually turned over to storage, but they make fine work areas too. Stone floors are easy to clean and age gracefully.

STAIR STYLE *below right*

Stairs can be visually arresting. Here, a simple change of paint colour and floor covering turns them into a feature. Opening up the area underneath creates extra living space.

BENCH MARK *right*

A wooden bench, simple panelling and natural accessories are all you need to give a hall a pleasantly rustic feel.

STORAGE IDEAS

- It may be possible to build a run of fitted cupboards or shelves in a wide hall or corridor. Stopping these short of the ceiling will help to preserve the original proportions of the space.

- If you are desperate for extra storage, and possess basic joinery skills, consider turning the space under the stairs into a series of pull-out cupboards and drawers.

- For stability, coat and hat stands should be fixed to the wall.

- A row of pegs is invaluable for depositing keys, bags, scarves and other outdoor accessories. Position some low on the wall for storing children's items.

- Keep shoes out of the way by storing them in a cabinet, or on a slatted shelf. This should be low enough to fit under hanging coats.

- Never store wet clothing and shoes in closed cupboards or drawers.

- Bicycles can be kept off the floor by placing the crossbar or front wheel on a wall-mounted bike rack. In a very narrow space, it may be possible to store one above your head by hooking it up to a pulley system. Store the helmet and reflective accessories nearby.

- Eyesores, such as pipes or meters, can be built into a cupboard.

CHAPTER EIGHT

GARDEN ROOMS

Blur the boundaries between the outdoors and inside by creating a gentle transition of colours and textures. Emphasize natural light, vary the flooring, carefully place generously-filled pots of flowers and shrubs in corners and use lightweight furniture to mark the change of use.

Space plants creatively, choose complementary containers and make a virtue of small spaces. Included here are ideas on furniture, outdoor lighting and plants. Open the doors and let the fresh air in.

Bringing the Outside In

We instinctively gravitate towards windows for good reasons: we are drawn to the light and, unless the window faces into a courtyard, we are seduced by the promise of a view or general activity beyond.

Windows also bring the outside into your home. When the sun is shining and the air is warm, open windows allow the sounds and aromas of the outdoors to drift inside. At other times, windows perform a protective function.

Use the same hard flooring inside and out to blur the frontier line where the two meet; plants may be arranged in containers on the windowsill, and rooms can be furnished with natural materials such as wood and wicker.

Most of us like nothing better than to sit and relax, work or eat by a window. Any type of window is suitable, as long as it has a reasonably low sill. The best ones are those which form a bay or some other enclosure, or tall windows that stretch towards the ceiling. Even the smallest window becomes a source of pleasure when it features a built-in seat.

A glazed extension or conservatory is the most dramatic way to bring the outside in. It is rarely a cheap option and needs to be designed carefully if it is to be comfortable all year round. However, the advantages of building a conservatory are that you will have more usable floor space, an increased sense of light, and it can transform the way you move through and use the rest of your house.

GREEN ROOM *left*

A luxurious sense of peace is created by surrounding outdoor-style furniture with houseplants in a variety of shapes and sizes. The cool, stone floor reinforces an outdoor feeling.

PANORAMIC TABLE *right*

It's a shame to cover up distinctively framed windows with blinds or curtains. Here, pots of tall geraniums ranged along a sill are a natural and colourful way to create privacy.

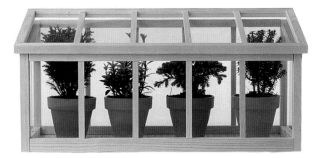

NATURE TRAIL

Nature can be an endless source of inspiration, even when you live in the middle of a city. Materials and objects which were designed to be used outdoors bring a rugged beauty to indoor spaces, while the decorative potential of fruits, vegetables, plants and flowers, has been recognized since the first still-life painters. These days, naturally beautiful objects have an additional purpose; they poignantly remind us that we live in an increasingly artificial world.

Although it can be heavy, expensive and difficult to lay, a natural stone or brick floor is a worthwhile investment, as it grows more beautiful each year, giving decades of virtually maintenance-free use. It might be more practical to use these materials on a smaller scale such as a small stone wall fountain in a conservatory. A feature in its own right, it will also humidify the air for tropical plants and provide the gentle sound of trickling water in the background.

Hardwearing fabrics such as hessian and canvas can make a successful transition indoors; their inherent stiffness makes them perfect for sail-like window blinds or as a wallcovering. On a smaller scale, they are often used to line baskets and to cover boxes.

Materials which were once confined to the potting shed can now be found in the smartest rooms. Unglazed terrracotta pots and dishes look equally at home on a dining table, while galvanized steel, still used to make watering cans, has a rigidity which is suitable for shelves and boxes. Even the humblest natural materials can be transformed with a little imagination. Try wrapping and glueing coarse jute string tightly around simple objects such as square or cylindrical cartons, or combining it with good old-fashioned brown paper when wrapping gifts.

The sturdy construction of many outdoor objects makes them eminently suitable for busy households. Shaded hurricane lamps and night-light lanterns are more stable than candles, especially where there are children around. The glass shades also magnify and refract the light in interesting ways. And a canvas tool bag makes a

brilliant beach holdall for several towels. The outer pockets can be used to store sun protector, water bottles and bathing suits.

A classic way to bring the garden indoors is the use of houseplants. Different varieties exist for many conditions, climates and budgets. They tend to have most impact when several pots of the same plant are grouped together on a surface; or when a single, striking example such as a standard topiary bush, or ivy trained on a frame, is treated as a piece of sculpture. Houseplants do not have to be large: a group of seedlings in a cold frame, or pots of herbs on a windowsill, have just as much charm. The key thing is to look after them: a humble yet healthy plant looks far more striking than any amount of struggling exotica.

Don't forget that, when flowers are out of season, fruit and vegetables also make inspiring table centrepieces. Instead of creating a mixed basket of fruit, try sticking to one variety for a homely look, or combining it with dried flowers and seed pods; apples and ears of wheat are a timeless harvest combination, while bright orange carrots and purple lavender clash creatively when placed side by side in terracotta pots. Fruit can scent a room too; oranges studded with cloves are a Christmas favourite, but you could also hang up strings of apple slices, or allow the sun to warm two or three quinces.

INDOOR/OUTDOOR FURNITURE

VERSATILE SEATS
opposite above left

A lightweight kitchen table and folding chairs can easily be lifted onto an adjacent patio for breakfast outdoors.

SANDY WHITES
opposite below left

A seaside holiday mood is evoked effortlessly by canvas-covered stools, striped and sheer fabrics, and a light-diffusing canopy.

OUTDOOR BANQUET
opposite right

A group of small tables creates a more informal setting than a single large table and is eminently suitable for entertaining outdoors. Tall metal plant stands and the shade of a tree help to define the dining area.

SUMMER COLOUR *left*

French windows are a smart yet practical way of linking indoor and outdoor spaces. Vibrantly-coloured wood and wicker furniture brings the colours of summer flowers such as geraniums and marigolds, into the house all year round.

LIVING OUTDOORS

Only the most hyperactive gardeners would disagree with the idea that outdoor spaces are for relaxing in; if you're lucky enough to have access to a balcony, a terrace or a garden, the chances are that a part of it, or all of it, is already set aside for eating and sitting in – even if the weather allows for such activities for only one or two months of the year. If you have children, it may be that the space is used primarily as an outdoor play area.

The best places to sit outdoors are those that get the sun, and are sheltered from the wind. In very hot countries, or at the hottest times of the year in more temperate climates, light or dappled shade is also welcome. The only furnishings you need are: something to sit on, be it a deckchair or floor cushions covered in sturdy canvas or cotton; and growing plants, preferably set at a variety of heights so that they seem to envelop you with their colour and fragrance.

A veranda, or a patio with a retractable awning, near the house is ideal. Outdoor spaces above ground level, such as balconies and roof terraces, can feel very exposed, but this is easily remedied by enclosing them with trellis panels.

If the sunniest spots are away from the house, then it makes sense to site your living area there. Create a sense of enclosure by adding a low wall of raised flower beds planted with aromatic herbs, or with a windbreak.

Eating outdoors with the sun beating down on your neck is far from pleasurable, but the magic can be restored by shading the furniture in some way. Unless your garden is very bare, you are unlikely to treat the furniture as a focal point, so choose designs which are made from

OUTDOOR LIGHTING

- Rather than attempting to light large areas of garden, which can make it look like a prison yard, use outdoor lights to highlight features such as trees, water pools and seats. The easiest way to do this is with spike-mounted directable spotlights.

- Wall lights are useful for creating background illumination on patios and terraces. Bulkhead fittings, which shield the bulb with an opaque diffuser, create less glare.

- Outdoor lights can be used to make the front entrance of your home more welcoming and secure.

- All outdoor lights should be corrosion-resistant and watertight, and if you are planning to site them away from the house, cables should be well buried.

LANTERN LIGHTS

Electricity is unnecessary when you light your garden with lanterns, candles and flares.

wood which will weather to a warm grey tone, or dark blue and green colours, as these tone better with foliage.

Children see outdoor spaces as somewhere to let rip, so a family garden or patio needs to be designed for boisterous activity and messy play. It is best to pave very small spaces, so that the children can ride bicycles and play ball games. Hard surfaces are also best for sandpits, so that any escaped sand can be swept up easily. If you have a larger garden, a grassed area is safest for siting climbing frames and a swing.

CLAPBOARD COTTAGE *opposite*

The right setting matters more than elaborate furnishings when you live outdoors. Virtually any kind of simple seat will do, as long as it is placed close to sun, shelter and greenery.

ELEMENTAL STYLE *above*

Dining by the water would be pleasurable enough for most people, but here the experience is made even more sublime with the addition of a generously-sized table, and director's chairs with tie-on squab cushions.

SMALL OUTDOOR SPACES

IN THE WOODS *left*

If you are lucky enough to have verdant surroundings, a terrace needs nothing more than comfortable furniture. Here, generously proportioned seats can be used both for relaxing and dining. A folding umbrella provides instant shade, and in the evenings, outdoor candles supplement light that spills from the house.

PRIVATE VIEW *above*

Balconies and other outdoor areas attached to the home make extremely good focal points and can be enjoyed even when you are indoors. Curvaceous wood and rattan furniture make a pleasing contrast to rectilinear metalwork and window frames.

ROMANTIC BALCONIES *left*

Outdoor living spaces don't have to be large; a small balcony can be just as inviting. A flowering creeper makes use of the wall rather than the floor. Furniture that blends in with its surroundings also helps to expand the space visually.

COSY CORNER *above*

Laying a square of natural matting is the quickest way to warm a stone or concrete floor below. For comfort's sake, leave enough room to stretch your legs, and choose a table that is large enough to take a tray and some reading matter.

DISPLAYING PLANTS

RAISED PLANTINGS

A wire plant stand *left* provides a stylish raised surface for displaying pots of primulas. The long and narrow shape of the etagère echoes that of a window box; but individual plants are easier to replace when it's time for something new.

below A metal etagère laden with vibrant orange pansies would liven up the dullest outdoor corner. Creating a sense of fullness is vital when you are making a container garden. To achieve this, plants must be watered daily and fed weekly during the growing season. Pruning them regularly encourages repeated flowering.

MEDITERRANEAN SETTING *right*

A southern European feel is conjured up on a shaded veranda by wicker armchairs, orange standard trees, pots of lavender and scented herbs in a lead trough. The texture of weathered terracotta sets off green plants perfectly: antique containers are expensive, but it's easy to soften new pots by painting them with diluted plain yoghurt or liquid fertilizer.

Where to Find IKEA

There are more than 120 IKEA stores around the world, with more opening all the time. You will find stores in the following countries:

Australia
Austria
Belgium
Canada
The Czech Republic
Denmark
France
Germany
Hong Kong
Hungary
Iceland
Italy
Kuwait
The Netherlands
Norway
Poland
Saudi-Arabia
Singapore
Slovakia
Spain
Sweden
Switzerland
Taiwan
United Arab Emirates
USA

ACKNOWLEDGMENTS

AUTHOR'S ACKNOWLEDGMENTS

I would like to thank IKEA UK for providing constant support and encouragement throughout this project. They championed its cause, clearly communicated IKEA's philosophy to the assembled team, and met our endless requests for products and information with unwavering courtesy and enthusiasm. My thanks also go to IKEA Sweden for giving us access to the company's picture archives.

For believing in the project and providing encouragement, thanks to Suzannah Gough, and at Weidenfeld & Nicolson: Michael Dover, Richard Hussey, Jenny Manstead, Jackie Strachan and Beth Vaughn.

For finding many of the wonderful images, I would like to thank picture researcher Nadine Bazar. Her talent for tracking down exactly the right image is awesome. Thanks also to Gareth Jones for his help with the picture research and to Ian Muggeridge for his expert handling of the text.

For working at the speed of light during the special photography sessions, my thanks go to curtain and cushion maker Robyn Rolls, furniture designer Richard Ward, decorative painter Nick Ronald of Grand Illusions, St Margarets, upholsterer Helen Leeson and the boys at Andy Knight Set Builders, as well as Claudia Dulak and Altan Omer for assembling the furniture.

Thanks also to Rosie Lakin; Asheem, Rohney and Sitaara Parikh; Ella Richards; Anita and Nina Wale; and Alkesh Woods for letting me empty their wardrobes and toy cupboards in search of props. To Nicolas Miller, for allowing me to photograph the inspiring home office on page 168-9, again. And to Brian Copestick and John Lakin.

My greatest and final thanks, however, are reserved for the friends who worked with me on this book, and who helped me through what were often difficult times. To Trevor, Fiona, Jo and Meryl: I made it thanks to your support and inspiration.

PUBLISHER'S ACKNOWLEDGMENTS

The publisher would like to thank the following for lending props used for special photography:

Pages 20-21 plate by Bill McCulloch, from Rebecca Hossack, London W1; 34-35 fire inset and tools, Townsends, London NW8; cushions and telephone, Gore Booker, London WC2; prints by Birna Matthiasdottir, Flowers Graphics, London E8; pressed silver accessories and silver-rimmed bowls and dishes, The Kasbah, London WC2; decanters, The Dining Room Shop, London SW13; table centrepiece, Rebecca Hossack, London W1; 36 television, Bang & Olufsen UK; stereo, Kenwood UK; storage boxes, Paperchase, London W1; 37 silver tray, tea glasses, lidded ceramic pots, wooden box and wire lantern, The Kasbah, London WC2; cushions, Gore Booker, London W2; 43 radiators, Bisque, London NW6; 106-107 prints by John Loker, Flowers Graphics, London E8; cup and saucer, Cath Kidston, London W11; 110-111 clothes by Factory Workers, London; hats by Fred Bare, London; *centre* clothes by CHRIS by Chris Mestdagh, Belgium; sweaters by Quinton & Chadwick, London N1; 117 *top right* print by Hiroko Imada, from Flowers Graphics, London E8; tissue box holder, Cath Kidston, London W11; 140-141 sink, bath, taps and shower fittings from Colourwash, London NW10; floor tiles from Criterion Tiles, London SW6; bath products from Natural Products, London NW6; 160-161 ski clothes and accessories from Snow & Rock, London W8.

PHOTOGRAPHIC ACKNOWLEDGMENTS

The publisher thanks the photographers and organizations for their kind permission to reproduce the following photographs in this book:

Pages 3 *bottom* VT Wonen/D Straatemeÿer; 10 VT Wonen/Hotze Eisma; 11 *top* VT Wonen/ Holze Eisma; 14-15 Belle/Simon Kenny; 16 VT Wonen/Hotze Eisma; 17 Dominique Vorillon; 18 DIA Press; 21 *top* Hotze Eisma; 22-23 Christopher Dugied/Marie Claire Maison/ Florence Sportes for IKEA; 24 Studio Verne; 29 Belle/Simon Kenny; 44 *above left* Elizabeth Whiting & Associates/Tim Street-Porter, *above right* Dia Press, *below left* Marie Claire Maison/ Tosni/Borgeaud, *below right* Marie Claire Maison/Tosni/Borgeaud; 45 The Interior Archive/Simon Brown; 46 *above* David Phelps; 47 VT Wonen/Hotze Eisma; 48 Peo Eriksson/ Creative Director IKEA, Michael Ekblatt; 48-9 VT Wonen/H Zeegers; 54 *below* Dia Press; 56 Studio Verne/Architects WAWW; 57 *left* Camera Press; 60 *below left* Dominique Vorillon/ Designer Kerry Joyce, *above left* Marie Claire Maison/Snitt/Rozenstroch; 61 Dreyer/Hensley; 62 The Interior Archive/Simon Brown; 63 VT Wonen/Hotze Eisma; 65 *below* VT Wonen/ Hotze Eisma, *bottom* VT Wonen/ D Straatemeÿer; 68 VT Wonen/O Polman; 69 Studio Verne/Architects WAWW; 70 Christian Sarramon; 70-71 David Livingstone; 71 Studio Verne/Designer Carlo Seminck; 76 Elizabeth Whiting & Associates/Tom Leighton; 77 The Interior Archive/Simon Brown; 80 Studio Verne/Architect Citerio; 81 *right* Elizabeth Whiting & Associates/Rodney Hyett; 82 *left* Christian Sarramon, *centre* Dia Press; 83 Abode UK/Eric Thornburn; 84 *below* Dominique Vorillon/Architect Tom Bosworth; 84-85 JB Visual Press/Horst Neumann; 85 The Interior Archive/Simon Brown; 86 *below* Lars Delsgaard; 87 Dominique Vorillon/Architect Dan Killory; 92 Christian Sarramon; 92-93 VT Wonen/ D Straatemeÿer; 93 Paul Warchol/Architect

Marco Pasanella; 94 *above* Camera Press; *below* Studio Verne/Architect Vincent van Duysen; 95 VT Wonen/H Schuurmans; 99 Hotze Eisma; 100 Marie Claire Maison/Dugied/Postic; 101 The Interior Archive/Simon Brown; 102-103 Marie Claire Maison/Tosni/Puech; 103 Hotze Eisma; 105 *left* Ianthe Ruthven, *right* Paul Warchol/ Architects Peter Forbes and Associates; 114 *above left* Marie Claire Maison/Hussenot/Puech, *below left* Geoffrey Frosh, *right* Marie Claire Maison/Tosni/Borgeaud; 114-115 VT Wonen/ D Straatemeÿer; 118 VT Wonen/ D Straatemeÿer; 119 VT Wonen/Hotze Eisma; 120 *above left* Elizabeth Whiting & Associates/ SIP/Snitt, *below left* Camera Press/IMS:Uggla/ Appeltofft; 121 *left* Marie Claire Maison/Dugied/ Postic, *right* Marie Claire Maison/Dugied/Postic; 125 *left* Studio Verne/Architect Jo Crepain, *right* Belle/Earl Carter; 127 *centre* VT Wonen/ D Straatemeÿer; 128 Marie Claire Maison/ Chabaneix/Puech; 130 Jerome Darblay; 131 *left* Elizabeth Whiting & Associates/Neil Lorimer, *right* Dominique Vorillon/Architects Jeffrey Biben and Peggy Bosley; 133 Marie Claire Maison/ Nicolas/Postic; 134 The Interior Archive/Simon Brown; 134-135 Robert Harding Syndication/IPC Magazines Ltd/Tom Leighton; 135 Jerome Darblay; 136 JB Visual Press/Hannu Mannynoksa/Designer Ristomatti Ratia; 136-137 Elizabeth Whiting & Associates/Rodney Hyett; 137 Mark Fiennes; 138 Arcaid/Alberto Piovano/ Architect John Winter; 138-139 VT Wonen/ D Straatemeÿer; 139 Paul Ryan/International Interiors; 142 Robert Harding Syndication/IPC Magazines Ltd/Jan Baldwin; 147 Hotze Eisma; 148 *below* Arcaid/Julie Phipps/Architect Tom Grodona; 149 *left* Homes and Ideas © IPC Magazines, Robert Harding Syndication; 151 Hotze Eisma; 153 Lars Dalsgaard; 163 The Interior Archive/Fritz von der Schulenburg (Andrew Wadsworth); 167 VT Wonen; 168 Studio Verne; 169 Ron Sutherland; 172 Marie Claire Maison/Dugied/Ardouin; 173 *right* Elizabeth Whiting & Associates/Dennis

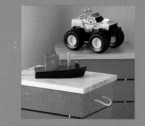

Stone/Designer Tim Thomas; 175 *left* Belle/
Petrina Tinslay/Architect Philip Diment; 176 *top*
VT Wonen/Hotze Eisma; 178 *below left* Christian
Sarramon; 178 *above left* Lars Dalsgaard; 179
VT Wonen/D Brandsma; 180 Elizabeth Whiting
& Associates/Tom Leighton; 181 *above* Lanny
Provo/Designer Dennis Jenkins/table and mirror
designed by Urbanis; 184 *left* Paul Warchol/
Mosely residence and studio, Architrope, *right*
Andy Glass/Designer Kate Fontana; 184 *centre*
Lars Dalsgaard; 186 VT Wonen/Hotze Eisma;
187 *above* The Interior Archive/Simon Brown,
centre VT Wonen/Hotze Eisma; 188 Marie Claire
Maison/Primois/Postic; 192 *above left* Abode
UK/Eric Thornburn, *below left* Marie Claire
Maison/Pataut/Puech; 193 VT Wonen/Hotze
Eisma; 194 Dreyer/Hensley; 195 *left* The Interior
Archive/Fritz von der Schulenburg (Dot Spikings);
196 *right* The Interior Archive/Fritz von der
Schulenburg (Richard Mudditt); 198 *above*
Elizabeth Whiting & Associates/SIP/Waldron,
below Marijke Heuff (Mrs L Goossenaerts);
198-199 VT Wonen; 208 The Interior Archive/
Simon Brown.

The following photographs are reproduced
courtesy of Inter IKEA Systems B.V. 1995:
Pages 8-9; 12; 19; 25-27; 46 *below*; 49; 52-53; 54
above 54-55; 57 *right*; 60 *above right* and *below
right*; 64; 66; 73 *centre*; 74; 78-79; 81 *left*; 82 *right*;
84 *above*; 86 *above*; 90-91; 97; 98; 111; 117 *below
right*; 120 *right*; 122-124; 129; 142-143; 146; 148
above; 149 *right*; 150; 162; 165 *top*; 166; 173 *left*;
174; 187 *bottom*; 189; 192 *right*; 195 *right*; 196
left; 197.

The following photographs were taken specially
for Weidenfeld & Nicolson by Trevor Richards:

Pages 2-3 *top*, *above*, *centre* and *below*; 6-7; 11
above, *centre* and *bottom*; 20; 21 *top*, *centre*, *below*
and *bottom*; 31-43; 50-51; 58-59; 64; 65 *top*,
above and *centre*; 88-89; 96; 97 *top*, *centre*, *below*
and *bottom*; 106-110; 110-111; 112-113; 116; 117
left and *above right*; 126; 127 *top*, *above*, *below*
and *bottom*; 140-141; 143; 144-145; 154-161;
164; 165 *above*, *centre*, *below* and *bottom*; 168-9
courtesy Nicolas Miller; 170-171, 176, 177 *above*,
centre, *below* and *bottom*; 178 *right*; 181 *left*;
182-183; 185; 187 *top* and *below*; 190-191.

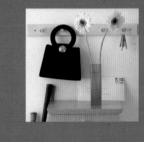

INDEX